I0639289

TIME TO
RISE

29 Soul-Stirring Stories of Personal Growth and
Professional Transformation That Will Help You
Find Your Purpose and Live Your Best Life

Created and Compiled by
DR. ANDREA PENNINGTON
Foreword by **SISTER DR. JENNA**, Director, Brahma Kumaris Meditation Museums

TIME TO RISE

29 Soul-Stirring Stories of Personal
Growth and Professional Transformation
That Will Help You Find Your Purpose
and Live Your Best Life

CREATED AND COMPILED BY
DR. ANDREA PENNINGTON

MAKE YOUR MARK GLOBAL

MAKE YOUR MARK GLOBAL PUBLISHING, LTD
USA & Monaco
Time to Rise © 2017 Andrea Pennington, MD, C. Ac.
Published by Make Your Mark Global Publishing, LTD

The purpose of this book is not to give medical advice, nor to give a prescription for the use of any technique as a form of treatment for any physical, medical, psychological, or emotional condition. The information in this book does not replace the advice of a physician, either directly or indirectly. It is intended only as general information and education. In the event that you use any of the information in this book for yourself, as is your constitutional right, the author and publisher assume no responsibility for your actions. No expressed or implied guarantee of the effect of use of any of the recommendations can be given. The authors and publisher are not liable or responsible for any loss or damage allegedly arising from any information in this book. All of the names and details have been changed to protect the privacy of individuals.

Without limiting the rights under copyright reserved above, no part of this publication may be reproduced, stored in, or introduced into a retrieval system, or transmitted in any form or by any means (electronic, mechanical, photocopying, recording, or otherwise), without the prior written permission of the copyright owner.

The scanning, uploading, and distribution of this book via the Internet or any other means without the permission of the publisher is illegal and punishable by law. Please purchase only authorized electronic editions and do not participate in or encourage any electronic piracy of copyrightable materials. Your support of the author's rights is appreciated. And karma will get you if you violate this anyway!

While the author has made every effort to provide accurate information regarding references and Internet addresses at the time of publication, the author does not assume responsibility for errors or changes that occur after publication. The author also does not assume any responsibility for third-party websites and/or their content.

Book cover design: Andrea Danon & Stefan Komljenović of Art Biro Network
Editor: Carol Taylor of Brown Sugar Books
Back Cover Photo Copyright 2017 In Her Image Photography www.InHerImagePhoto.com

Library of Congress Cataloging-in-Publication Data
Library of Congress Control Number: 2017918265
Time to Rise
Publisher: Make Your Mark Global, LTD
Fernley, Nevada
p.274
Paperback ISBN 978-0-9992579-0-6
Ebook ISBN 978-0-9980745-9-7
Subjects: Self-help

Summary: In Time to Rise, Dr. Andrea Pennington presents 29 inspiring tales of people from various backgrounds and cultures who didn't let tragedy and defeat hold them back. These stories cover events ranging from painful divorces to health issues to professional struggles. What these people all have in common is how they used these problems to transform their lives for the better.
Printed in the USA & UK

MAKE YOUR MARK GLOBAL PUBLISHING, LTD
USA & Monaco
Time to Rise © 2017 Andrea Pennington
For information on bulk purchase orders of this book or to book Dr. Andrea or any of the authors in this book to speak at your event or on your program, call +33 06 12 74 77 09 or send an email to
Andrea@MakeYourMarkGlobal.com

TIME TO
RISE

CONTRIBUTING AUTHORS

Julia Aarhus - Karan Joy Almond - Dr. Janet Anthony

Gegga Birgis - Sarah K. Brandis - Roméo Cournal

Missy Crutchfield - Dr. Debbie Engelmann - Dr. Gayle Friend

Gitte Winter Graugaard - Lene Kirk - Deri Llewellyn-Davies

Todd Malloy - Elaine Mendoza - Malcolm Out Loud

Marijana Popovic - Siena Pennington - Geneviève Pépin

Jesper Pilegaard - Lorena Plæhn - Susana Silverhøj

Joana Soares - Katrine Spiegelhauer - Dr. Jill Stocker

Carol Taylor - Yvette Taylor - Sólveig Þórarinsdóttir

Leslie van Oostenbrugge - Evakarin Wallin

DEDICATION

This book is lovingly dedicated to the countless souls who feel lost, unloved and confused.

May this book help you reconnect to who you really are

May you find peace and hope

May you claim this moment as your time to rise

CONTENTS

Foreword

The book in your hands, and what your eyes are about to witness, are stories that will help us gain deeper purpose about our own lives. It is a culmination of life-changing experiences from luminaries who share compassionately their truths to power. Our lives have never been more complex and yet at the same time we are being offered an enormous opportunity to rise to our highest selves. With factors ranging from God, soul, our bodies, social norms, and acceleration of technology, we could all too easily find ourselves more distant from our personal truth and power.

What we need aren't sweet anecdotes or quick fixes, but rather a deep inner focus on our true intrinsic worth, power, courage, and inner peace. However, we will need to remain consistent and open to diversity.

Dr. Pennington has gathered a myriad of voices from various backgrounds and perspectives that offer us room for growth and a wider understanding. I believe when we open up to listening and learning from others, we become better people. Looking for new conversations and new tools becomes a means for creating a newer and better future.

Time to Rise offers deep insight that sheds light not only on what is, but also what we can be, if we push ourselves further. You will gather tools on how to better heal from coaches, therapists, and healers who share with the readers how they broke through their own limitations and blockages. Each and every human being gets a call when it is time to rise, however, we get distracted on too many occasions and forget to heed the call.

Right now is the time for each and every one of us to rise and be true to who we really are. It can be scary, but most of us realize that we must no longer be silent, we must no longer just fit in, we must bring the best of ourselves so the rest of the world can benefit.

From my personal reality of being raised by an Indian father and an African mother who was orphaned at age seven, to running top nightclubs in South Beach and Key Biscayne, Florida, to racing cars and living a life of a young woman who could get just about whatever she wanted, there was that call that told me it was time to rise! I discovered that there was so much more to learn, to let go, accept, forgive, and amplify.

Regardless of where you are at this time on your journey, I believe the personal stories and reflections in *Time to Rise* could become a prescription to help everyone gain insight to move with courage, to heal, elevate, and activate.

Sister Dr. Jenna
Director, Brahma Kumaris Meditation Museums
Host, America Meditating Radio

Introduction

Do you feel there is something inside of you — a dream, a message, an idea — just bubbling, tingling, gnawing at you? Perhaps it's the fantasy of living in a new country, of finally feeling free to express yourself in art, or the desire to stop living a lie and 'come out' as the real you. If you have a something that keeps you up at night, occupies your mind daily or creates a sense of angst that you can no longer deny, then this book is for you.

Time to Rise includes a collection of personal stories from 29 coaches, mentors and healers who dug deep within themselves to strike out on a new path in life. Some of these change makers were no longer willing to be bound by the confines of cookie-cutter careers so they broke free from a life of conformity and took flight as entrepreneurs. Some are showing true courage as they challenge societal norms or family traditions to elevate their standards to live life and love on their own terms. While others demonstrate the immense power and resilience of the human spirit as they show, time and again, that they will not be held down by others, illness or rules. They prove that it is possible to bounce back after illness, financial adversity, divorce and other hardships or loss with grace. And so can you.

You are more powerful than you may realize. All of the abilities you will read about in *Time to Rise* are also within you. These inspiring stories of transformation will motivate you to cultivate your courage, strength, and confidence to boldly rise up and soar to new heights in your life, relationships, business and personal wellbeing.

I am truly proud to know these authors as they have inspired me, too. Their willingness to be vulnerable and share their truth has given me an even greater motivation to spread their messages of healing, hope and happiness around the world. Because our world needs these true stories to remind us of our collective and individual strength.

Millions of people around our beautiful Earth now recognize that we are One, we are an interconnected family of incredibly unique, dynamic and resilient spirit beings. As the global awakening spreads we are being called to share our realizations to inspire and empower others to wake up and rise up with integrity, authentic power in a peaceful rebellion.

By bringing this book to the world, we are coming together to provide encouragement and support to you, too. By simply reading this book you are now connected to a global community of change makers who are consciously choosing peace, integrity, authenticity and love as their motivation. You are no longer alone.

May you find the encouragement and determination to live your life, as your authentic self, with confidence, courage and compassion. May you embark on the next phase of your life journey with joy and conviction. Now is your time to rise.

— Dr. Andrea Pennington

TIME TO
RISE

1

RISING TO THE OCCASION

Rising on the Road Less Traveled

Malcolm Out Loud

My greatest fear was to wake up one day and find that life had passed me by. What if I did not take the opportunity to rise when it was my time? But how would I know when it was my time? Where was the fork in the road that would say: "Now! Take that one!" I seemed to be waiting for something to hit me over the head. I knew I didn't want to wait for a "now or never" moment. I wanted to be the one who decided when and where. But it doesn't work that way.

There are divine moments that interrupt your life. At the time, you don't fully realize how important those moments are, but the choices you make now will decide the path forward. I am reminded of the great poet Robert Frost and the words he wrote in his 1916 poem "The Road Not Taken."

> Two roads diverged in a wood, and I—
> I took the one less traveled by,
> And that has made all the difference.

It is truly amazing how one simple yes or no answer can set you on an entirely new path. I was enjoying the advertising business and I was damn good at it. But I'm one of those cats that get bored with the status-quo. Boredom forced me to reconsider my world of work, but I was pulled back in again and again as the money accumulated in my bank account. What was it that I feared if the security blanket in my bank shrunk? And so, I waited.

With little warning, the voices of change grew louder and I knew it was time—past time—to make the leap from the boardroom. It was as if I received a call to return to the imagination and vision of myself as a kid in grade school where I knew I would make a substantial difference in the world. I was always told it is best to look before you leap. The training of caution seemed so alien to my current knowing—the rising up of my authentic self—and I struggled to erase that caution in order to negotiate my future. I had a choice to make. Do I begin to imagine that future—whether it be a run for political office or creating the media to make a difference—or do I deflate and come back to the status quo? My new awareness said the latter would be the death of me. As I saw my road—the one that led to the business of radio and media communications—the demons of doubt multiplied and got louder. What if the radio business doesn't like me? What if I don't connect with people? What if I can't fill the airtime with intelligent conversation? What if I can't make a living? For all the 'What if?' reasons that exist, there is a 'So What?' moment. As my rise began, I became more and more attuned to the "road less traveled" theory that sustained me.

As my work evolved, I came to call this a 'Brink Thinking' moment. I had such a moment in June 2010 when I rose from the boardroom to the microphone. It had become apparent to me that most of the brilliant minds were not out on the front lines where they could impact the next generation. Secondly, there was a major shortage of good news stories in the media sphere and virtually no problem solving or solutions driven editorial out there. So yes, this was obviously a road less traveled, but an important road that could make a huge impact on young and old—just as I had dreamed as a young boy.

Following my choice—the cutting of the corporate cord—I was living in two parallel universes. At least it seemed that way. One universe had me covering the news cycle on national radio. As a news commentator and host, there was no shortage of bad news to go around—I know because I reported on it. But something was missing. There is far too much truth to the phrase 'If it bleeds, it leads.' They say bad news sells, not positive news or encouraging stories that improve our lives. I beg to differ. It was late 2015, everything was humming along, yet I had no idea that within months I would choose once more to go on the other fork in the road and to rise above the mundane news. I have founded a podcast network, then a talk radio network, and then a full platform of writers, authors, radio and podcast hosts and video YouTube stars. The America Out Loud Platform was born in April of 2016. My focus was to "let the silent voices be heard," and boy are they being heard!

In order to present a quality and riveting message, I had to ask myself: 'What separates those at the top of their game from the rest of the pack?' First there is the passion. Many people have passion, but these same people often underestimate the details. Yet that is where the sweet spot lives. My job was to find those people who combined their passion with a strong ability to communicate their core concepts. My created universe centered on all these exciting and inspiring stories of people that were finding themselves on the brink of some life decision that might transform their life, and that would ultimately give hope back to the human race.

Now it is time to carve out your unique path forward. And yes, oftentimes, you need to reach for the road less traveled by.

5 Pivotal Life Lessons on Your RISE to Greatness

1. Remember to RECHARGE your soul along the way

Our souls become battered over time, abused and often confused. Are you just existing or are you reaching for a higher purpose in your life? You can't turn off the world of reality while you imitate a deer in the headlights. It is important to breathe and check in with your soul with an honest reality check about who you really are and what you want from this lifetime you've been gifted. All too often our minds become entrenched with the negative energy around us—you can change this.

Take a close-up look at your surroundings and begin the small steps to changing the things that you know deep inside must be changed. Remove the negative forces around you that are stifling you. You must cleanse your mind of all the negativity that occupies your soul. Start anew. Wake up to a different morning routine. Turn the technology off. Step outside and breathe. Attach yourself to the idea that you are starting anew on your terms. This is your life and your opportunity to rise. Be honest. Be authentic. Be at peace. Be thankful for your life. Let your gratitude and praise soak in your thoughts and radiate in your soul.

2. REFOCUS your priorities from time to time

Does your daily regimen support your yearly plan, and does your yearly plan feed into your life plan? We get lost with all the distractions and urgent matters in our lives. All too often our 'true' priorities are at the bottom of the list. The key is to get those priorities back to the top of your list. Step back from all the clutter and think it through, write it down and create your yearly plan and the daily action steps—the milestones that will take you there.

Take a lesson or two from the great basketball superstar Michael Jordan: "I've missed more than 9000 shots in my career. I've lost almost 300 games. 26 times, I've been trusted to take the game-winning shot and missed. I've failed over and over and over again in my life. And that is why I succeed."

If the RISK outweighs the reward, then reconsider the journey—find another way or abandon the idea. If the REWARD exceeds the risk involved, then don't let anything stop you from exploring the unknown. You can do it.

3. It may be time to REEVALUATE your relationships

Negative thoughts create inferior results. It's like everything else in your life—your mind takes the shape of whatever you feed it. Those relationships that are constantly in your ears with gossip and bad news… you need to drop them like a hot rock. Positive people hang with positive people and get superior results. It's said that we are the average of the five people we hang with. It is time to take inventory of who those five people are.

Keep it positive, don't allow the negative energy to consume you. Read a motivational book, subscribe to some positive blogs, listen to some uplifting music. Positive intentions translate into positive results. Seek out positive reinforcements for your lifestyle. They can be people you don't necessarily always agree with, but who you can have an honest disagreement with, without repercussions. If you can capitalize on strengths and weaknesses that complement the ones you possess, the relationship will have more potential.

"We can improve our relationships with others by leaps and bounds if we become encouragers instead of critics," says Joyce Meyer.

It's easy to be critical of others in the decisions they make, but we rarely ever know all the circumstances surrounding a decision. Be sure that you have all the facts and then offer alternatives while being respectful of the decision. Before you criticize someone, walk a mile in their shoes.

4. Stuck in neutral? It happens. REENERGIZE your mission

The same daily regimen will produce the same daily results. We are mostly creatures of habit. Face it; you probably order the same food, drive the same roads and call the same people day in and day out. Your routine may be holding you back. When your days become too predictable, your creativity and desire to improve will almost certainly become stagnant.

Turn your schedule upside down if you're seriously looking for a different outcome. Refresh your mindset by breaking out of your routine. Start with the simple things like food choices, travel choices, people choices before you consider career and life changes. A different structure to your daily routine will result in a new and improved structure to your overall life. The question to ask yourself is: 'how can I advance my dreams forward?' A good idea will remain only a good idea unless you can advance it to a great idea! Moving your agenda of dreams forward is a sign of greatness. Question everything around you, both good and bad. Look at the alternatives—this is not the time to play follow the leader, it's the time when leaders step up to the challenge at hand.

5. Never compromise who you are. It is YOUR RISE to greatness

Do what you love in life and life will love you back! Greatness is habit forming and if you work at it day in and day out, your moments of greatness will multiply. Never be afraid to reinvent yourself. Where do you want to be five years from now? Give this some serious thought (and write it down). What steps will it take to get you there? Break those steps down into micro-steps that are manageable. Find the passion in your life by engaging in the areas that excite you. Most importantly don't change for change's sake— do it because you truly desire a new and improved life.

It's impossible to get excited about your life and your work without passion. Passion can only come from within; it's an intense emotion consisting of feeling, enthusiasm, or desire for something better. Without passion, details suffer, the quality is hindered and the overall outcome diminished. Passion is that feeling of unusual excitement or just having a positive affinity towards life. When we are passionate about our life, it almost always results in a greater satisfaction. Doing what you truly love in life is a gift.

"The world is in need of a new generation of leaders. Leaders who have the courage to break through the boundaries and question everything around them. Society is yearning for bold and enthusiastic women and men to provide the necessary leadership that will be required for the next leap forward." This is even truer now than when I wrote it in 2007. The world needs people of passion, intellect and the ability to communicate. The fresh air of those three elements helps both our contributors and our followers to rise with us.

The history of human experience is full of tales of success and failure and amazing stories of perseverance. What separates the average person from the exceptional? I talk about this when I describe 'What makes a Brink-Thinker?' I find that too many people are content with letting others create the BIG IDEAS. They are naturally discouraged by the world around them, but every one of us is capable of achieving extraordinary feats. For this process, I suggest what I call "BRINKSTORMING." Here are the Golden Rules for the process that can help you speed up your RISE:

1. Your boundaries are 100% self-imposed. Be in charge of your own thoughts.

2. Never settle for an average idea. Be exceptional and bold in your thinking.

3. Don't follow, lead. Find alternative methods to break through the clutter.

4. Question everything, the obvious and the not-so-obvious. What if?

5. Uniqueness is the golden rule. If everyone else is doing it, then don't.

6. Don't panic when the idea seems absurd. Absurdity is oxygen for high flyers.

7. Take your idea to next-level thinking—all the way to the BRINK.

Brink Thinkers are people like you and I who have learned to nurture, persist and expand our thoughts to create unparalleled results. Many of your everyday ideas have the potential for greatness. The secret is to take that thought, that concept, that idea, all the way to the BRINK!

BRINKSTORMING™ is all-encompassing

The brink of societal change. The brink of courage or bravery. The brink of helping others live a more purposeful life. The brink of lessons learned and now valued. The brink of peace in the world. The brink of death just before life. The brink of undying determination under great obstacles. The brink of victim turned victor. The brink of possibilities and not despair. The brink of saving lives. The brink of invention. The brink of positive attitudes that give hope. The brink of never stopping until the realization of your goal.

If enough people get bold, choose their road, carve out their place in the world, then the rising will spread far and wide. And it will. Guaranteed. There is a time for everything. A time to wake up. A time to make your bed. A time to eat dinner. A time to meet friends. A time to work. A time to breathe. A time to make the leap. A time to stop complaining. A time to live your life. A TIME TO RISE.

About the Author

Malcolm is the driving force behind and Founder of the America Out Loud talk radio network, a motivational speaker, author, TV presenter, and a trained life coach. His nationally syndicated radio show 'MALCOLM OUT LOUD TALK' can be heard daily on talk radio, on podcast sites and streaming radio. Malcolm Out Loud TV is the groundbreaking digital news magazine that brings a fresh perspective to a world vying for quality programming. 'BRINK of Greatness' is focused on the human spirit with tools and life lessons that will drive your own agenda for greatness.

Connect with Malcolm online:
www.malcolmoutloud.com
www.americaoutloud.com

It's ALL right

Carol Taylor

"The greater the obstacle, the more glory in overcoming it."
~ Molière (1622-1673)

As I go through this journey called life, I have discovered that it's ALL right. I've discovered that we have to be okay with where we are; and that really, it's our only option. We have to make peace with where we are *before* we can go anywhere else. We are all at different places on this journey. Some are in good places and some are in not so good places. Once we become conscious of where we are and accept and even appreciate it, only then things can change. So let me say it one more time because it is, so important…it's ALL right.

My "time to rise" started on August 22, 2011. On that day, I found myself in a dark place, with my head in my hands crying. I was at the very bottom with nowhere to go but up. Despair, grief, guilt, blame, worry, hate, and anger flooded me as I sat in the clinic's waiting room. I was in complete and utter fear. I was the only one there so I knew the news was really bad. It's not usual for the medical office to close for lunch and leave you sitting there. I had an envelope in my pocket and in that envelope was my stamped divorce papers. It verified that, on that same day, I was officially the single mother of two young boys Zack and Jaden, ages eight and fourteen. These two young boys, were depending on me.

My senses were fully active and I was forced into the present moment in a very profound way. I was intensely aware of every sensation. I was sweating, my jaw was tight and aching, and my stomach was in a huge knot. I could hear distinctly, the receptionist shuffling papers and talking on the phone. There was calming music playing on the speaker system, and the hum of the ventilation was loud when it kicked in. I noticed every painting on the wall and they were vibrant with color. I could see people walking on the sidewalk outside and it almost seemed like they were moving in slow motion. The phone rang again, and the receptionist took a moment to push back her hair before answering it. The smells were intense as well. The perfume of the lady who walked past me on her way out was jarring. The odor of the freshly painted walls mixed with the sharpness of the sterile cleanser was intense. The door to the examining rooms seemed to swing open in slow motion when my doctor called me into her office. I followed her and my senses were still on high alert. I sat down in the chair across from her and there was an awkward silence. "The tests came back positive. You have breast cancer. I'm so sorry," were the words that came out of her mouth. Then she stood up, walked over, and hugged me.

It's been more than six years since that day and I have been rising and learning ever since. Like I said, there was nowhere to go but up...well there was but I didn't want to go there. I knew it was a place from which I would never return. I had come to at a fork in the road. I had a choice to make on my journey—#1 to give up and slowly die or #2 to learn and grow and live in a way that was healthy, authentic, and from my heart. I chose option #2. There was no other choice. I had two very important reasons to face this obstacle, my boys. They needed me and I needed them.

Interestingly, my life seemed to unfold in three-year increments. I had spent three years trying to make a toxic and dysfunctional marriage work. I had taken three years to get my divorce finalized. Then I spent three years after that focusing on my healing. It took three years to write, publish, and market *Smiling Single Mom—It's ALL Right!*, a book about my journey. My next three-year cycle is starting as of August 2017 and I can't wait to see what unfolds in the next three years. How's that for a dramatic backstory?

In those six years my precocious fourteen year old grew up and is now twenty. He finished high school and was accepted into college where he completed a two-year program in Instrumentation Engineering Technology. He finished last April with honors and has just started his dream job as a programmer for a local business. Within the next few months he will be in his own place, starting his own adventures as a young contributing member of society. I couldn't be more proud of him.

My sweet little eight year old is now fourteen and inspires me every day with his achievements, growth, and his amazing heart. He is excelling in music and last year he won the Don McCleary Music Award at his school. This year he transferred from the middle school to the high school and within the first two days his math teacher requested that he go up a grade. He was nervous and excited but was up for the challenge and so far he is near the top of his class academically. He is also actively involved in the Cadet program and just finished his Silver level for the Duke of Edinburgh program. My sons make me super proud every day and I am so glad that I chose option #2. Kindness and love can change the world and I am reminded of this often as I look at my boys.

Next I would like to touch on the 5 main principles that helped me shift into a healing mind space.

1. **Fill up Your Bucket First**: Take care of yourself. If you are feeling like you need something, you probably do. It's not selfish to take care of yourself, it is the only way to rise. Listen to your body. It knows more than you give it credit for.

2. **Find Balance in Your Life**: Givers who give and give, until you have nothing left, need to make time to balance your body,

mind and spirit. There is abundance everywhere, you just need to learn to tap into it.

3. **Look Within**: See where you need to grow and do it before you are *forced* to do it. Notice the small subtle hints. You don't have to wait for the mountain to come crashing down on you. We all have different journeys and our chosen path is right for us.

4. **Listen to Your Heart**: If you don't want to do something, don't do it. Don't guilt yourself into that something. Listen to your impulse, your instinct, your intuition and go with that. If it sounds or feels good, do that.

5. **Let Life Unfold Naturally**: Those are the doors that open easily for you. If you are trying to kick down a door and make something happen, it means you aren't supposed to go in there. It's not for you. Walk away. Another door will open. Walk through that one.

Remembering these 5 essential principles helped me to shift my perspective and truly thrive.

I would like to share with you, a letter that I wrote to my dad when he was suffering with anxiety and depression.

Dear Dad:

Believe.

As you know, I like to express myself through words. And as I sit here sipping my tea, I feel the need to listen to my heart and write you this letter. I love you and I believe in you and I am one of your support people. In the same way that you were there for me—as you loved me, believed in me, and supported me when I was sick—I am there for you. I wanted to share with you the six things that helped me stay strong, hopefully they can help you too.

1. **Believe**: I believed with all my heart, mind, and body that I would get through cancer. I had a dream and a burning desire to achieve it!

2. **Support**: I reached out and trusted in my support people—my family, my friends, and my doctors. I surrounded myself in a world of healing and a bubble of love. I saw all the beautiful things around me and was very thankful for them.

3. **Intuition**: I listened to my heart. If something felt wrong, I listened. This is why surgery and chemo felt right for me but radiation and five years of drugs did not. I did the Sway Test on many things and today I have a pendulum that helps me tune into and listen to my intuition.

4. **Cause**: This was the hardest step of all for me because it meant digging into my feelings and asking what I could do to fix things. For me, there was a lot of resistance that I had to let go of because negative emotions cause stress, and I think stress was the cause of my illness. Everybody has a different cause and only they can find it. I support you in finding your cause.

5. **Prevention**: Ask yourself, "what can I do" to keep this situation from occurring again? This is where your action plan comes into place. For me, my work became a goal to reduce the stress in my life in many ways, and I am still learning new things every day. I do things every day to fill up my bucket—I exercise, I eat healthy foods, I take time for myself—because I realized that if my bucket was empty then I was no good to anyone. I could write for pages and pages on this step because it's my favorite and because it's ever changing.

6. **Surrender**: Forgive and move forward. Have faith and know that you are surrounded by angels of all kinds. As the saying goes, "Let go and let God."

I hope this helps you in some way. Just know that the boys and I, and many other people in your life, love you, believe in you, and support you. Now for my question—do *you* believe? Because I think that miracles happen for those who believe.

Much Love,
Carol

Now for the story of my tattoo. I'd been thinking about getting a tattoo for many years and had designed it in my mind and on paper, but was always afraid to act. Fast forward to one year after my diagnosis, I decided to mark the day by stepping out of my comfort zone once again by getting a tattoo.

The day after getting it, I wrote in my journal: I did it! I got my tattoo. It's amazing and they did such an awesome job. All the elements of the tattoo symbolize something very important to me. The red heart represents Love and Trust, and the pink rose represents Growth and Beauty. The rose has two petals, which represent my two boys.

The butterfly signifies Freedom and the colors, on its wings transition from blue to purple to red. Blue for Zach, purple for me, and red for Jaden. The heart shows the inner peace and strength that I feel. It symbolizes intuition, emotion, transition, and relationships. The single rose is without thorns and represents admiration, gentleness, gracefulness, appreciation, joy, sweetness, success, and strength. The butterfly is a sign of transition, celebration, lightness, soul, faith, and change. Mine is a morph butterfly so it's even more beautiful. And beauty, by the way, is in the eye of the beholder. For me, getting this tattoo was something that I had always wanted to do but was afraid to do. I have thought for many days and put a lot of consideration into what it would look like. This is a manifestation of years of thought, so it was especially important to me. I Love, love, love it when we step out of our comfort zones amazing things can happen.

As I mentioned earlier, the number three has been significant to my life. Here are my three affirmations and the steps that I continuously work on to become more authentic.

1. **I Will *Awaken* to My Authentic Self:** I will use engaged inquiry practices—like meditation, breathing, silence, Pilates and the Sway Test—and I will listen to the answers. I will ask, I will listen for the answers, and I will act on them.

2. **I Will *Align* With My Authentic Self:** I will be aware of the choices I make and the subsequent results. I will look at my values and see if I'm aligned with them. I value love, trust, growth, beauty, and freedom. I will face my negative and limiting beliefs and release them.

3. **I Will *Create*:** I will look for the oneness in everything and I will use my energies to create in my life and in other people's lives. I will create wonderful relationships, financial success, and I will surround myself with all things that make me feel good. I will write and sing and dance and play, and I will enjoy something beautiful about every day.

I'll end this by saying again that I've discovered that it's ALL right. What will the future bring? I don't know and I'm okay with that. I'll figure it out as I go and so will you. Thank you so much for coming on this journey with me. I hope the letter that I wrote my dad when he was struggling with anxiety and depression resonates with you, as well as the story of my tattoo. And may my three affirmation steps to becoming more authentic inspire you on your journey. It's your journey, live it the way you want to. Without you it would not be the same.

Thank you. Where there is love, there is beauty. Much Love and Light to you! And remember… It's ALL right!

About the Author

Carol grew up on a farm in Alberta, Canada. After graduation she moved in with her future husband. They were together for twenty-six years and in that time they co-created two marvelous boys and a lot of wonderful memories. Carol has held a variety of jobs, but enjoyed her work as a lifeguard and swimming lesson instructor the most. She received her Bachelor of Education in 1995 and is currently a teacher. She enjoys spending time with her boys, going on adventures, writing, reading, cooking, hiking, biking, living in the moment, loving, laughing, learning, drinking tea, meditating, doing Pilates, Facebooking, spending time in her yard and in nature.

To get in touch with Carol, email her at taylorc@live.ca. To follow her blog or order copies of her book, *Smiling Single Mom - It's ALL Right*, check out her website at www.smilingsinglemom.ca

Hooray for the Grim Reaper!

Karan Joy Almond

Melanoma! Hallelujah! Hooray for the Grim Reaper, I thought as I sat across from a doctor who was struggling to find the right words to ease the blow of her diagnosis. My experience as an Oncology RN told me that an appropriate response to a cancer diagnosis should be initial shock, tears, anger, denial, bargaining, and a plethora of emotions that eventually lead to acceptance of the fight ahead. But I was unable to muster a single tear, or a single fear, in that moment.

You see, I had already prepared for war and gone to battle for my health. Although I understood that my whole life had been leading up to a systemic crash, I was weary with the expectation and no longer had the will to fight. So, this melanoma thing was the best news I had gotten in a very long time. It meant the suffering had an endpoint. It meant I could stop fighting. So, while this compassionately thorough doctor discussed the possibility of post-surgical treatment, I was already considering how I would handle it without appearing suicidal and getting myself committed to the Psych Unit. I could tell my reaction was not common by her slow and deliberate choice of words. I suspect that she may have thought I was in shock. I said little but smiled and nodded as she discussed what to expect and the possibilities during my course of treatment. It was clear that she suspected metastatic melanoma due to the length of time the lesion had been growing.

A friend had noticed the lesion on my thigh and urged me to make a dermatology appointment. I honestly hadn't given it much thought as I went to see the dermatologist. I explained that I was only there because a friend insisted I come. I told her I had first noticed the lesion about two years earlier so I was sure there was nothing to be concerned about. The doctor decided to biopsy the lesion and also a second site for what she termed "kicks and giggles." Turns out both were identified as melanoma. So now what, should I kick something or was it really okay to giggle?

I managed to remain in "appropriate patient" mode and said that I was not open to chemo or radiation. This was met with, "We don't have to make that decision today. Let's just get through the surgery and then we can have that discussion." Win-win! My family knew that my oncology experience left me feeling that the treatment for cancer was often much worse than the disease. They knew I would not choose chemo. When I was seventeen, my father didn't chose chemo for pancreatic cancer and, certainly, my family would understand that a metastatic melanoma prognosis was poor and that I didn't want to add suffering to my remaining days by watching them deal with the side effects of chemo. So I left the office knowing that I would undergo surgery and that would give me a legitimate argument for why I was not willing to give any other treatment a chance.

Three weeks later, I'm sitting in that same office prepared with my speech about why I would not be choosing further treatment. This time though, I really was in shock as the doctor gleefully uttered the words "clear margins," "no further treatment," and "you are one lucky lady." What a cruel trick! I was numb except for the feeling I would crumble under the weight of this "good" news.

On the way home I stopped at the park and headed to a quiet grassy hill where reflections of trees dancing on the water had often given me moments of serenity. I needed to find some peace. I needed to understand. I was angry. I didn't know how angry until I let out the pain in a scream that had been hiding for years behind anger. My entire life had been a tug-of-war with my autonomic nervous system. I lived with a constant looming feeling that at any moment I would have to fight or flee. I had been dealing with my illness for so long that I'd lost the desire to fight but there was no fleeing from it.

I felt the weight of it all but in a different way. It was a realization that it was not coming to an end. That may have been the single most important come-to-Jesus moment of my life. It was most certainly a pivotal moment in my illness. For years, I had dealt with the neurological effects of lyme complex, mold toxicity, and mercury toxicity. I went through over thirty doctors and specialists before I found one who would diagnose and treat me. I was on thirty-six medications and using a walker to hold up my 110 pound frame, when I met him. Because lyme is not readily accepted as a chronic condition that can affect the skeletal system, the nervous system, and the organs, diagnosis and treatment are often delayed. It is difficult to get a lab confirmed diagnosis and the insurance companies frown upon doctors treating a clinical diagnosis. Lyme goes into the chronic form within weeks to months of exposure for many people.

Initially, I went to war with the illness and tried to fight it without a proper diagnosis, which leads to confusion and frustration, since every practitioner has a different perspective. I had diagnoses ranging from Multiple Sclerosis based on white plaques identified in my brain to Munchausen's Disorder, based on a medical recommendation that any doctor who continued to allow me to believe my symptom complex was bordering neglect or malpractice. Eight long years later, I was finally diagnosed and properly treated by a doctor who I remain with today.

While I could probably write an entire book about the illness, my purpose here is to explain how that illness served me. You read that correctly. Without the illness, without the melanoma, I am not certain how thick of a board upside the head it was going to take to get me to listen. I needed to stop. My whole life had been about being prepared to fight or flee and I was uncertain how to deal with my new awareness. I understood that this was a spiritual growth opportunity but I had no tools to make a plan for that.

I wondered if I should go back to church or visit an ashram. Heck, perhaps I should go to Machu Picchu or engage in shamanic rituals. Of course, none of that was possible because I could barely get up and down my own stairs. Episodes of severe exhaustion, debilitating weakness, and phantom pain came on frequently and without warning, so I couldn't make plans to travel or even commit to local events. My ex-husband was tolerant and gave me the luxury of being able to stay home and attend to my health. But this took a toll on family and friends alike—they couldn't stay in that space with me. My family went on with their lives. My pre-illness friends all but disappeared.

For many years that sense of betrayal and abandonment was a crushing pain that I could only articulate through anger or tears. It only served to wound them and created more distance between us—emotionally and physically. My deepest regret is my family's suffering. Back then, I did not know how to change any of it, I only knew my desire was to change all of it.

It has been over seven years since the melanoma diagnosis and I would love to say I have perfected the process and healed my lyme disease. I have not. But I did begin to actively participate in a different way. I realized that while I couldn't control my situation, I was in control of how I chose to respond to it. I started putting one foot in front of the other and simply taking whatever action was in front of me, while also honoring my need to take a nap or skip an outing without feelings of anger and isolation.

I became a biohacker, joined every Facebook healing group, and read every off-the-grid treatment I could find. In the middle of my search, I found Biological Dentistry. I decided to have my mercury amalgam fillings removed after learning about the damage mercury can do to the lining of the stomach and the nervous system. The period between 2011 and 2013 was a long, complex set of interrelated problems, but the end result was eleven root canals followed by multiple surgeries to try and treat the chronic osteomyelitis infections that attacked my jawbone after those root canals, all in what would turn out to be failed attempts to save my teeth.

In 2013, I met a biological dentist who would change my life in ways I couldn't possibly imagine as I sat in his consult room and discussed extracting all eleven teeth. The recurring infections had left my jawbone and facial bones fragile and pockmarked, like Swiss cheese. My father had lost all of his teeth before age thirty-five and he was dead by age thirty-nine, so the prospect of losing my teeth terrified me to my core. But I was desperate. By now, I wanted to live. I wanted it badly enough to do whatever was necessary to regain my health and participate in a meaningful life.

In 2014, he extracted the entire upper right quadrant. Shortly thereafter, the dentist offered me a part-time job with his practice as a Patient Ambassador. During the next two and a half years, I had multiple surgeries and started the process of getting implants. I worked in his practice for three years with no teeth in my upper right quadrant. I had lost too much bone for a partial denture to be functional or comfortable. While I was never comfortable with not having teeth, allowing patients to see me like that was actually a gift for most of them. Many times, I would meet with a patient who was anxious about losing a tooth until they became aware of my dental surgery.

I began the twelve-month implant process in the fall of 2016, which included harvesting a graft from my hip bone to help reconstruct my jawbone. While I had seen slow but steady improvement in my symptoms and functional abilities, the graft surgery took a toll with a six-week recovery and a recurrence of lyme symptoms.

In December of 2016, my husband told me he "needed some relief" and for him, that meant separating. I understood. I already felt guilty that our marriage had become passionless because of my fatigue and pain, as well as my fear that my many different infections could be transmitted during sex. Just prior to that decision, I was offered a full-time position in the dental practice. I was over the moon with excitement and felt that finally things were going to change for the better. Then my husband, left for good. He was done. By February, I was working full-time at a job I had passion for, but my husband and son were gone.

Skip ahead to August, 2017. Without realizing it, I had poured all of who I was into a job that gave me purpose. But the dentist's office manager, who self-identified as his gatekeeper, was suspicious of my easy camaraderie with the dentist and his staff, which made me a target for her emotional abuse. I knew I had to leave.

I felt abandoned and betrayed, again. My body had betrayed me with illness. My father's death, my husband leaving, my friends distancing themselves physically, and my emotionally distant or angry children had taken a toll... Fear of betrayal had been with me for so long, I wore it like a second skin.

I now see there will never be a moment when I will "arrive" and life will finally be easy. The key to getting through it all, for me at least, is perception. It's how I choose to see it, and in that "it," how I see myself. It's how I choose to define it, and in that "it," how I define myself. There is no good or bad, right or wrong. It is simply another opportunity to see what I am made of. This realization led me to understand and begin to accept that my life-long challenges have been uniquely purposeful. Every time I recall a particularly difficult and painful event, I can see now that it led me to the next level of self-discovery.

This realization, the understanding that my thoughts and fears were creating the very level of hardship that I thought life kept imposing upon me with every challenge, started with the melanoma diagnosis. It took me this long to realize that cutting out that melanoma cut a chink in my armor—it made me vulnerable by forcing me to accept that there was more I was supposed to do.

Buddha tells us that suffering is necessary. We cannot know joy without it. I have come to believe that humans avoid suffering so much that we suffer in order to avoid suffering. I have suffered and I will suffer more. But I know with every fiber of my being that the suffering will be temporary if I choose it be, and it is an opportunity to create a new reality. One that is closer to allowing my internal beauty to be expressed without all the conditions we place on expressing ourselves.

I am nearing closure on my dental reconstruction. It was brutal, but I would not trade the illness or the dental hell for anything. They made me strong. They made me who I am. I know that every person on my journey, whether they were present in the way I wished or not, was there at exactly the time I needed to learn the lessons they would bring to me. For that, I am grateful. There is beauty in the chaos and there is clarity in the confusion when we can let go and trust that we really do not have to do it all alone or figure it all out before taking action. Sometimes we have to jump without knowing where we will land. We simply need to know that the parachute is on our back and the rip cord is in our grasp!

About the Author

Karan Joy Almond is a retired RN who believes the pursuit of physical, psycho-emotional, and spiritual wellness is the right of every human. Her thirty-five years of experience in healthcare, both as provider and patient, has taught her that while licensed providers can be a godsend to patients with singular concerns, their services often do not address the patient as a whole person. As a result, the information and treatment can be fragmented and fail to present all the options. Karan has studied dozens of healing modalities, both traditional and alternative, and specializes in identifying how to integrate multiple treatments to biohack health. She is available for individual consultation, workshops, and speaking engagements.

Visit her online at www.facebook.com/JoyLightWorks to request a free twenty-minute diagnostic interview.

Playing Dead to Stay Alive Made Me "Sassy"

Dr. Debbie Engelmann

The lessons presented to each of us by the life we live, whether labeled in our mind as good or bad, are supreme healing gifts for the human soul as well as our entire society. The language of lessons is not the language of lesser or better, but rather of limitation and opportunity. To see lessons as "gifts", one must first decide to open their eyes wide enough to see them. My soul's deepest wish is you gleam some tidbits of insight from the words that follow that help you become your "genuine" self. To be drawn, in one way or another, to something bigger than a simple vision. To discover and understand what empowers you so deeply you finally recognize the dynamic person you already are. The caveat is this—becoming "sassy" is a requirement. This means you'll need to learn how to "sculpt a soulfully sassy you." Being sassy is all about finding and releasing the power of your soul's deepest personal truth to confidently begin living your life *on your own terms*. When you do, you'll join an ever-expanding tribe of people who have chosen to move beyond their life stories to heal themselves, society, and the world.

There's a chance you are thinking *Wow, no way. I'm not sure I can do that.* You *absolutely* can! There isn't a single painful "life story" that cannot be healed. If you focus on healing consciously and authentically, you can surmount anything. I experienced this firsthand. It took me quite some time to even attempt being sassy because I feared being physically and/or emotionally harmed. I wasn't afraid of the dark—I was afraid of who was in it. As a child, my fear caused me to continually freeze—to stand still and play dead to stay alive. Being sassy during those years would have been like throwing gasoline on a fire. Deep in my "child's soul", I knew

I needed to hide until I was safe, and I couldn't put on my first pair of sassy pants until I was. When that time came, I learned how to be bold, spirited, and yes, very sassy. With therapy and the love of those around me, I trusted myself enough to begin my own personal healing journey.

During those dark years, my four-year-old self easily accepted my trauma-induced hyper-vigilant behavior as being normal because it kept me safe. My extreme sensitivity to sound and movement was comforting because that increased alertness warned me of any potential danger that might lead to abuse. Unfortunately, over time, this hypersensitivity caused a great deal of physical damage, fatigue, and exhaustion which took years to heal. These types of damaging effects from trauma are now known as Post-Traumatic Stress Disorder (PTSD). Occasionally I still overreact to unexpected loud noises—thirty-years+ after the abuse ended. I remember feeling terribly trapped, abandoned, unloved, and utterly alone for the first twenty years of my life. Back then, falling asleep could have dangerous consequences so I learned to live on very little sleep and ended up developing insomnia. Today, staying asleep has become less challenging through my bedtime meditation practice. While writing this chapter, I realized that when I get out of balance I begin to judge others and myself very harshly. My thinking becomes black and white—things become right or wrong with absolutely no middle ground. I become defensive and blind to my own truth. When this occurs, my healing technique is to get out in nature and slowly walk in meditation to ground and release all judgments against myself and others. It works beautifully.

Paulo Coelho wrote, "It takes a huge effort to free yourself from memory." Because of my creative type mind, most of my childhood nighttime dreams were actually nice. Reality was anything but. I remember when I opened my eyes each morning, my heart would flutter because I knew it was imperative to pay extremely close attention to everything happening around me. As mentioned earlier, back then it was paramount for me to vigilantly watch for any hint of anger that could quickly turn into my being emotionally, verbally, and physically abused—again. As I reflect on those times, I find it exceptionally illuminating to realize when something does not move, we humans (especially adults) tend to stop looking for any movement. This tendency appears to help "playing dead to stay alive" create more "moments of safety" for abuse victims—it did for me. I firmly believe I avoided some abuse in this fashion because it allowed me to hide beneath my Harry Potter cloak of invisibility to remain safely hidden until my time to heal arrived. Healing from physical, emotional, and sexual abuse doesn't mean the abuse and its effects never existed. It simply means I choose to no longer allow those damaging abusive memories to control my life.

A larger question comes into play at this point. How do we heal from painful memories? The essential first steps I used in healing my memories of abuse and/or hurtful memories was to try to fully grasp and understand what my personal truth was deep inside my soul—about absolutely everything. Here's where being sassy had its biggest impact. By using raw, brutal, brazen honesty I discovered the *truth of who I was and what my core beliefs were*. This was the toughest part of my healing. I had to find enough courage to look deep within myself and uncover all the truths I was hiding. This is where our personal power lives. We must each choose how to use this power whether it be competitively or to love and live life without judgment. The power within the soul craves meaningfulness and purpose—it loves without limitation.

Life is full of paradoxes, humor, and change. During my healing journey, I learned how to own my life rather than run away from it. I struggled with not becoming a victim of my circumstances until I discovered how totally *addicted* I was to being a victim of my life. When I became aware of this, in a flash I mustered up enough gut-wrenching strength to proudly put my sassy pants on. I deliberately used my anger to save myself—along with Brené Brown's books and classes. Through my study of the effects of shame and vulnerability, I consciously realized how much anger was bottled up deep inside me. I chose to love my anger rather than to try and destroy it. I cursed, beat pillows, kicked trees, swore worse than sailors ever have, screamed as bloody loud as possible, skipped rocks on the lake as far as I could, and other things I won't mention. Eventually, I heard my soul say, "Sweetie, it's time to pull yourself together." But the devil in me kept whispering, "Debbie, you're not strong enough to withstand your memory storms." So, I dug deeper into my truth and discovered "I was a storm—the storm of change." The wind no longer blows hard enough to stop my transformation.

Both authentic power and choice have their roots in the deepest core of our being. They cannot be bought or hoarded. People who choose to work with their authentic power are incapable of making anyone or anything a victim. What we humans tend to perceive as being unsurmountable, very rarely is. Choosing to be a victim of our "self" or our story limits transformation. Why does one person get up when they've been pushed down, and others don't? First and foremost, they *chose* to get up. They probably worked hard to not fall into the "false glory" of victimhood where they could blame life and other people for everything that happened to them. Victims tend to not hold themselves accountable yet they excel at "pointing the finger" at others. It's easy to hide behind victimhood and not move forward and avoid truth.

Conscious healing and empowerment brings all aspects of our human form into balance while it helps us move through life with a healthy body, honest emotions, a clear mind and a free-flowing spirit full of our authentic soul. My personal healing regime includes daily exercise, quiet-time, meditation, good nutrition, and long walks in nature. Quality sleep is a critical element of self-care that hugely impacts our physical, emotional, and mental well-being. The most powerful conscious healing event I've experienced to date was a 5-Day Silent Retreat with Santikaro, a teacher of the Buddha-Dhamma tradition, who founded Liberation Park in Wisconsin. During this retreat, I went so deep in my soul I found who I was buried beneath all the rubble. It was here that I touched my soul for the first time—where I cradled and healed my years of grief—where I forgave my perpetrators. It was in this most sacred place of "me" that I found the courage to let my stories go. Shortly after I let those memories go and discontinued seeing myself as a victim, I decided to begin my doctorate programs in natural healing to learn how to help others heal emotionally, physical, and spiritually. This is my passion. My practice continues to be a significant part of my personal healing while allowing me the opportunity to guide others as they move through the tangled maze of emotions and fears during their personal healing journey.

To heal, each of us must become cognizant of what we feel emotionally – especially if we try to manipulate ourselves or others. Emotion physically affects every cell of the body–not just the mind and heart. This is why honesty is very important – it doesn't cause damage. An example of a truly self-destructive habit would be becoming a "caretaker." Caretaking is very different from care-giving. Care-giving has no second agenda. Caretaking does. I learned this type of hyper-vigilant behavior from my narcissistic parents. To stay safe, I put my feelings and needs aside and took responsibility for the feelings and needs of others. I tried to fix them. Bluntly put, caretaking was actually how I made other people feel responsible for me. Unknowingly, I had learned to give others everything they wanted so I could at least be seen by someone. In return, they gave me the love, approval, and recognition I so desperately needed. I rescued people, people-pleased, flattered them with false compliments and made others' wants, needs, and feelings more important than my own. It was within a simple "ah ha" moment that I realized the trap I had fallen into. It took time and patience to learn how to authentically love others. But as my trust of people grew, I found I no longer needed that type of false attention from others to feel fulfilled. I now give to others what is left over after I have given to my most precious possession—myself.

One thing frequently occurs during the healing process but first, I'd like to pose a question to you. Do you consider yourself to be teachable? Are you honest with yourself? To achieve a balanced life, telling the truth to "self" is paramount. To be able to tell this type of truth to our soul, we must first become an "empty cup". Here's an illustrative story.

Once upon a time, a business person seeking enlightenment went to a Zen master. While waiting for the master, the individual became impatient and began tapping their foot while repeatedly looking at their watch. When the master walked in and offered a cup of tea, the individual took the cup and critically looked at the old man and said, "I want wisdom, not tea." The master smiled and started to pour tea, and he poured and poured, and he poured some more. The cup overflowed spilling the tea all over the person who angrily jumped and said "What's the matter with you old man? The master smiled and said;

"It is impossible to fill a cup that is already full.

Your mind is already full.

Only an empty mind can be taught."

To be aware and live in truth, we must each take a hard look at our assumptions because they can become our greatest obstacles.

When we hold onto an assumption, we are not teachable. In order to change, we must empty our cup. In order to see the world truthfully, we must be willing to see the world differently.

Our mental filtering system tends to distort our perception of reality. What we think of as "out there" is pretty much a huge mirror reflecting your filtering system right back to you. It is an energy system fueled by action and reaction. You have a thought and you seemingly interact with someone or something and then react to their reaction. It's a play being played out within the mind—a drama of life being hashed and rehashed. The truth is—there is no one else out there; it is all a projection. To achieve personal freedom, we must accept that "out there" is merely a reflection of what is going on inside. *Accepting* the fact that there is no "out there" and taking full responsibility for our pain and limitations is a courageous act. That bravery will be richly rewarded with an empty cup to begin learning how to live with clarity and truth.

A client once asked me a powerful question: "When you made the statement yesterday about my health, as you put it, "how you normally don't see people work on so many areas as I am...how does this happen? The person I was created to be has been locked away for so many years I don't even know who will emerge when we are done."

My answer:

"You are creating your own health, in whatever form you need it to be. Herbs and lifestyle changes work on the physical body to remind it how to function correctly, while flower essences release the subconscious emotion based issues. I, or any healing practitioner, could apply the exact same technique using the exact same words to multiple individuals and the outcome would be different for each person. The true source of power behind healing depends on how much the individual desires to heal. You came in with an agenda of "I'm doing this— it is time. And you did."

This client's "cup was empty." True healing began when she decided her healing would happen. If she had wanted me to be responsible for her healing, it could not happen. True healing is only accomplished by the person doing the healing. *I just happened to be the guide.*

I've learned a thing or two since beginning my personal healing journey and deciding to open my natural healing practice. Most importantly, my healing practice has taught me that lies, whether deliberate or unconscious, have many variations-truthfulness has none. My abuse taught me the value of using words to say nothing at all and silence to explain everything. Brene Brown said something I continued to remember on a daily basis: "When we deny the story, it defines us. When we own the story, we can write a brave new ending."

It's "Time to Rise" and write your new story—just remember to keep your cup empty.

About the Author

Debbie Engelmann, known as Dr. Deb, is a Doctor of Natural Health and Traditional Naturopathy, an Herbal Practitioner, and author. She is the founder of her natural healing practice, "A Well-Tuned Soul", which you can visit at (http://awelltunedsoul.com). Her author website located at (http://dengelmannauthor.com), contains her creative writings, book publication updates, and various thought-provoking essays, prose, and poems birthed from her childhood stories.

Her passion is to guide and advocate for the lost, forgotten, and ignored people—to help them find safety, health, and wholeness. She believes her educational background is what the stuffing is to a Thanksgiving turkey – the yummy part that makes everything else taste wonderful.

Rising Up

Gegga Birgis

I was about twelve years old when I crawled out of my sleeping bag, got down on my knees, put my hands together, and started to pray. I don't remember what I prayed about, but I was hoping that no one would see me while at the same time wanting everyone to see me. This was during a school trip and everyone was hiding in their sleeping bags after a ghastly ghost story told by one of the grown-ups to scare us.

Maybe I was praying for protection from the ghosts; I don't remember. But I felt there was someone out there I could turn to—God, Jesus, or angels—that I hoped was listening. It's been forty five years since that day, but I still remember the feeling of wanting to show that we could turn to prayers and/or a higher power if we needed. Even as a twelve year old I wanted to connect to that power. As a child I often prayed but wasn't much for churches. I was bored at Mass didn't like hearing about how "sinful" I was. My parents were far from religious and Sunday mornings they were often "hung over" because of the "festive" night before.

My prayers focused mainly on asking God to help everyone feel good, yes everyone in the whole world and especially not to let anyone suffer from hunger or war. Clearly, I was a savior at heart. I was very sensitive to people's feelings and I couldn't stand seeing other people suffer, especially if the suffering was because of another person. I still feel the same way, I often have nightmares and get depressed when I see something horrible in the news.

That dream of wanting to save people stayed with me into adulthood, which is why at twenty-one I became a registered nurse.

My other dreams where to have a cute husband, exceptional children, a big house and a great car. My dreams were all fulfilled.

I juggle my life without knowing the outcome.

Before I moved out of my parent's house I fell in love with a man who had drinking problems. I lived with him for twenty-two misunderstood years. In that relationship love was hardly expressed and the words "I love you" were never said to me. My fear of being rejected was so strong that I didn't even dare to ask my husband about his feelings—or express my own. I ended the relationship when I finally realized that I had a choice in my life and there was no sense in holding on to a bond that was holding me down and keeping my soul in chains. I had of course done my best in trying to change my partner, by using many different methods, at times alternating between grumbling, and tantrums, and being cute and sexy. I also tried staying busy by working all the time, trying to be the perfect homemaker. Neither worked. After I managed to get myself out of that dysfunctional relationship, I chose to love another man with a drinking problem. Of course, I tried to save him as well. I didn't succeed that time either. Partner number two had a beautiful daughter during our relationship—a huge surprise for him—and for me since I wasn't the mother of the child.

At this time in my life I was starting to finally understand my codependency, my fear of being rejected and my need for love. For a long time, I thought my job as a nurse and later a midwife where my calling. My "ability" to be codependent was useful in my job as a nurse, since other people's suffering kindled the savior in me. I excelled at helping others feel better. And their gratitude nourished my soul. Some of them even said I saved their lives. This type of gratitude helped me forget the measly paycheck I received each month. But I was still putting myself last. This pattern became a trap that I'm still struggling to get out of.

What is most important to me?

Where would I be today, if I had listened to my father's advice, after the financial crises in Iceland in 2008. He was constantly emphasizing (and still continuous to) how much better I would be off, financially if I had gotten a job in Norway as a nurse. The salary was higher there and a lot of Icelandic nurses were moving to Norway, where they could choose between many promising job opportunities. The problem, at that point, was that it was no longer my dream to be as a nurse. I didn't listen to my father's advice, I seldom did as a child and I wasn't going to start now in my fifties. My dear father didn't understand me. He was brought up fearing not having enough money to get by and therefore a high salary was his main concern—not to be happy in your profession. I finally resigned as a nurse shortly after the financial crisis in Iceland and decide to try my luck in the art world, after all, I had a BA degree in Art.

"Be the change you want to see in the world!"

Gandhi's insightful words did not yet have a special meaning for me. But in time I realized how this advice was not just a powerful way to happiness—it is the only way!

At this point in my life, I was divorced, lonely, unhappy and sometimes feeling like a victim. I read the books *Conversations with God* by Neale Donald Walsch (there are nine in the series) and they saved my soul and CHANGED EVERYTHING! I learned that when we deal with difficult changes in our lives and we don't want to go through the same suffering again and again, we have to change the way we look at life and also how we react to it.

I took part in my first retreat with Neale in 2008. There I heard Neale quote the Buddhist Thích Nhất Hanh's words, which forever changed my life. "If you smile five times a day for *no reason*, you can change your life in ninety days!" In other words, life is all about your *perception* of events in your life not about the events themselves! The message was crystal clear, the creative power lies within me and nowhere else. This was my aha moment! Let's try smiling when something bad happens.

But I wondered, how is it possible to see gifts in something emotionally painful? I asked God to explain that to me. Now I want to be clear about something, when I talk about God, I'm not referring to some guy up in the clouds. I'm talking about creation power itself, EVERYTHING THAT IS—you and me included.

I knew it would be difficult to follow Hahn's advice without some kind of (magic) tool to help me. It was then I had a great idea. I had some years earlier made a prototype of a piece of jewelry, that makes you smile. After I returned to Iceland I started to develop it further. I wanted so much to save the world. My fellow Icelanders where depressed and angry after the financial crash and in need of something positive.

When I finished the piece, which I call "an instrument of joy" I named him SMILER. To me he was a savior because he reminds us that we are The Creators of our lives—whether we like it or not. I felt like a genius and now the only thing that was missing was spreading the news and the world would happily embrace SMILER. Reality was, of course, very different. The route wasn't easy. In general, people's reactions were positive, they thought it well made, and the idea behind it noble. This was in part because of what I wanted it to do for people, but also because that part of the earnings went to charity.

SMILER is a beautiful pendant that can be worn by men and women of all ages. Then why didn't it become a runaway success? Why didn't shops clamor to sell it? Why didn't airlines want to sell it on flights? I comforted myself with Brian Tracy's philosophy—that with every no you receive you get one step closer to a yes. Deep down I knew the answer—I didn't want to sell SMILER as just another piece of jewelry. He is too special for that. He has a message to convey—to remind us that we are Powerful Creators with our minds, with our words, and in our deeds. We all have the ability to be powerful masters and to create a compassionate and happy life for ourselves with the right mindset. He was also created to tell us we are all one, so you *should give with joy what you want to receive*. SMILER needed a different kind of venue to get his message across. I began introducing the SMILER philosophy in lectures and courses and we had a very positive reaction every time.

It's now 2017 and I've been following my dream for nine years. My thoughts are sometimes fearful and give me reason to question myself. Aren't there lots of people with similar goals getting better results than I am? Would it be best for me to stop all this hard work and get a regular job? Every time I'm about to give up because my goals seem unreachable, an angel in the form of a person appears to give me new insight about how to continue. One of these angels is Bjarney Lúðvíksdóttir who offered to create the website for SMILER: smiler.is. This became such an inspiring project in every sense of the word. My art studio was filled with the funniest and most creative people and they all wanted to models for SMILER in my advertising. I experienced even more adventures with Bjarney, traveling with her to India, where she was working on a documentary film about girls that were survivors of acid attacks. I honored these girls as "Smilers" and invited them to participate in a workshop on SMILER philosophy and I donated all proceeds from selling the piece to them.

Andrea Pennington is another angel from heaven. She came into my life when I was in dire need of inspiration. To be able to teach, guide, inspire, and comfort—all at the same time—as she does, are brilliant skills I really do appreciate. I needed a mentor like her because she reminds me that I always have a choice about what I do and who I want to be. "Do you want to put your focus on your paintings or into promoting SMILER…or do you maybe need to take a break?" What freedom!

I often wonder if I should quit pursuing my dream, because being a pioneer with no money to back me up and working alone can be exhausting. And to feel you have lots of good ideas but no time or money to follow them through, can be frustrating. Therefore my solution these last few years has been working as much as I can as a nurse in a Psychiatric ward. That in itself has taken a lot of time and it has also taken its toll on my health and well-being. I lost focus on my dream.

Change the idea of God and everything will change.

I had one of many conversations with a patient of mine recently. She was anxious, hopeless, and felt unworthy, and wanted to die. She had tried taking antidepressants and going to therapy but nothing helped. During our conversation she mentioned a higher power. I asked if she believed in God? "No, definitely not!" she said angrily. "God is not good because he accepts suffering and even in many cases innocent children are involved." I sat with her for a long time and tried my best to paint a different picture of God. While we were talking I noticed a sparkle of understanding in her eyes. Her anger subsided, her mind had opened, and I could sense hope and peace emerging.

For God's sake and for so many miracles stories I have witnessed in my work as a nurse, I've decided to "rise up" again and, to "crawl out of my sleeping bag" like I did when I was twelve. Out of fear of rejection, I usually advertise my lectures without mentioning God. But after seeing the change in my patient I want to talk about this peculiar *God* even more openly than before. I want to follow my deepest desire to change people's perception of "God." I want to take this image of a "vengeful" entity we are taught to love and to fear and analyze his existence because I have questions: It says in the Bible that we are made in the same image as God. But what if God is something totally different to what we have been taught? What if we have misunderstood him and his message the whole time? What does it mean when religions say we all have the knowledge/kingdom within us? Does our perception of God have everything to do with how we see ourselves and other people and the world. We have been taught (and we believe) that God punishes— it is understandable that this belief might make us think it's okay punish ourselves as well as others. I believe we deserve something much better—something more loving and inclusive!

Nine years after my SMILER idea was born, I am still asking myself why am I still pursuing this dream? Does it matter to the world? What's in it for me? It hasn't made me rich *financially*, but honestly, that doesn't matter to me. The dream itself is more important. The question is, where does it lead me next? I can visualize a strong image for SMILER in the future, where he can flourish as the bearer of love, creativity, joy, and happiness. I create my own life and I have all the power within that is needed to make my dream come true, because I AM God (ok, not totally, more like a cell in his body) and I'm a Smiler within, a Powerful Creator… just like you!

About the Author

Gegga Helga Birgisdottir created a magical tool that turns on people's Spiritual Power and helps ease their Suffering. It's an Instrument of Joy and she named it SMILER. She is the author of the book Smiler Can Change it All. She is a nurse at the Psychiatric ward at the University Hospital in Iceland. Artist, NLP practitioner-coach, Speaker, NADA acupuncture therapist, and Midwife. Gegga has a passion to create workshops were she mixes spiritual wisdom and science into a potent cocktail, and the results are remarkable!

Gegga was born and lives in Reykjavik, Iceland. She has two wonderful grown up kids and a few sexy exes. She says everyone can be a Smiler within.

You're very welcome to visit: www.smiler.is, www.gegga.is

And contact: www.gegga@smiler.is

The Voice

Gitte Winter Graugaard

When I was pregnant with my first daughter I often thought back on my own childhood. My parents had done a wonderful job raising me. They taught me to believe I could shoot for the moon. They picked me up when I fell, and cheered for me when I succeeded. They still do. I thought if I could remember and decipher how they brought me up, I would have the recipe for a perfect motherhood.

I wrote down some of the memories to the child I was carrying. As the stories grew into tales, an old childhood dream of becoming a writer came back to life. My husband was all ears when I read them to him in the warm summer evenings in Croatia, where we had gone as lovers to grow into a family. As I write this I can still hear the background music of singing cicadas, smell the waves rolling to shore, and feel the warm summer breeze on my arms. Three years later those stories would turn into my first children's book and become a symbol for me to never stop believing in my dreams.

As I analyzed my upbringing I kept hearing a familiar Voice ringing in my ear. I knew The Voice so well, and now as I consciously tuned into it I wondered where it came from and what its purpose has been in my life. That was when I realized how important understanding the origin of The Voice was to create the recipe of the kind of mother and woman I wanted to be.

When I started wondering where The Voice had originated my first thought was that my mother had (somehow) plugged in a radio channel inside my mind. In my teenage years, her voice was always in my ear, and it came in handy so many times. For instance, I would be with my friends at a party. Something would happen.

Someone would be too drunk, pick a fight, do something stupid, inappropriate, or even dangerous. I would tune into myself and listen to what I, for many years thought was my mother's voice, and ask for advice. The Voice would then tell me what to do. It would get louder depending on the importance of the situation or my actions. I can't begin to describe how much The Voice meant to me as an adolescent and in my twenties as I struggled to figure out what life was all about. Once I understood the connection between my mother and The Voice I wondered what had been her mission to teach me?

In the eighties when I grew up, my mother was a strong feminist who fought for equality among genders. Today I know that she urged me to believe that I can do anything I desire and even make a difference in the world. She taught me to fight for what I believe is right and to treat people with respect and kindness. And she praised me more for bringing home the friendship award than medals for academics or sports.

My next revelation was figuring out that The Voice has multiple channels. Not only had my mother successfully planted her channel in my mind, she'd also opened networks for other close relatives. My father's Voice was broadcast in a mindful, loving, and patient way. He is the most intelligent man I know, and also the most present. When I'm asked who trained me in mindfulness, my father always comes to mind. His Voice, when it's broadcast in my ear, is always kind, but also very ambitious. Still today I often hear this question from his radio channel: "Are you sure you have done all you can to solve the problem?" In high school when I had trouble with classes, I would look to him for advice. His home office was filled with the familiar scent of coffee. I'd stand behind him, gently put my chin on his shoulder and wait for him to finish writing, so he could help me. Sometimes he didn't even have to say anything because it was already transmitted to me. I would then leave quietly inspired to work harder.

My sister also has her own channel. I only need to close my eyes to hear her nudging me to see things from more perspectives, to be patient, and know I will always have her shoulder to cry on. I also hear my grandparents. Although they are now in heaven, I can talk to them and they comfort me through their vibration or Voice. Something interesting happened after they went to heaven: Their voices and vibrations changed. They became less fear-based and more love-based. I often reflect on what we can learn from that about fear or loved-based living.

Sometimes several voices will battle inside of me at the same time. One particular inner drama played out just a couple of months before we moved to Croatia. It was fueled by the sudden epiphany that corporate life wasn't really for me. I was twenty-nine years old, had recently graduated (rather late) from Copenhagen Business School and had high ambitions to become a successful brand manager of a multinational company. But after only eight miserable months at an advertising company my body was screaming, my heart was aching, and my mind was going crazy. One rainy evening as I rode my bike home from work through the streets of Copenhagen, with tears streaming down my cheeks, I knew I had to find another path to follow.

I came home to my husband. We had met seven years before and had just gotten married. He was, and still is, the love of my life. That night I told him that I had to quit my job. Of course, I was scared and worried. So many voices were shouting inside me. But one Voice was so strong that I knew I had to listen it. I told my husband that the time had come to live our dream of going abroad together. I also told him I wanted to give birth to his child. Then something amazing happened. As I have experienced many time before and since, when The Voice is very strong and I listen to it, magic very often happens. The universe opens up to me and helps me reach my dreams. Three weeks later we found out that I was pregnant, and one happy week later my husband came home with an expatriation contract to work in Croatia. Those two years were followed by another two years in Canada. We left Denmark the two of us and returned home four years later with two small girls in our arms. One born in Croatia, another in Canada.

Becoming a mother made The Voice even louder. In those four years abroad on maternity leave I had many conversations with it fueled by anxious thoughts about my career or rather the lack of it. With the birth of my daughters The Voice had miraculously moved into my heart. I still don't know how. And as I wondered if I should go back to work or stay at home with my daughters, My Heart kept repeating, "Stay with your girls. They need you. You need each other. You'll find a way when the time is right. Don't worry." I'm forever grateful that I listened to my heart.

As my daughters grew up I wondered how on earth my mother had managed to transmit that Voice to me. When I asked her she looked at me with puzzled eyes. Because much has happened in her way of raising me that she has not been conscious of. I can see it when I ask those deep questions to try to understand the meaning of life. In the realization that my mother wasn't consciously transmitting The Voice in my mind, the next big revelation came to me. It must have been there naturally from birth. And if that is so, then everybody must have a Voice inside of them. One passed on from previous lives through the soul and then affected by their environment. Now if that's true, why do so many people feel lost in life? Why is it that some can't even hear their voices anymore?

The difference between those who can hear it and those who can't is that some of us have been trained our entire lives to listen to it. Some have known The Voice when they were kids and have sadly lost touch with it. That doesn't happen overnight. It happens bit by bit when you stop listening to it and is often caused by those closest to us, who themselves sadly have lost touch with their voices. In the beginning when we start to lose The Voice, it will scream at you and conspire with your body for attention. Just as it did the night I rode through the streets of Copenhagen. If you allow this to continue, the emotions and senses will become numb, and after many years of numbness, we might end up with stress or even worse, depression.

If you stay true to yourself, you will heed The Voice. But because it often encourages us to make hard choices that come with challenges, many people unfortunately refuse to listen, out of fear or because the pain of change is too overwhelming. I now understand that without courage and belief it is so hard to be true to your Voice. When we decided to go back home to Denmark, some difficult years would follow for me and The Voice as I tried to settle back into society. To my surprise I was offered a job almost immediately. My brain (and most people around me) said, take the job but My Heart started crying. The new position would require a forty-hour work week and a long commute. I did not want to leave my daughters in someone else's care for so many hours a day.

Luckily a friend offered guidance. She knew how to listen to different voices. She calls her method Deep Democracy. In my case it was a democracy of inner voices. She helped me speak to the voice of My Brain and separate it from the voice of My Heart. When they both talk at the same time it can be very hard to hear what they are saying. Sometimes the most frightened voice screams the loudest, which can make us think that we should listen to it, even when it is based on fear. The minute I started separating The Voices, I could so clearly hear My Heart sing again. It sang the most beautiful song to me and healed the fears of my brain.

Even though I often felt the odd one out, my choice to once again stay home with the girls and work part time on becoming a writer was so true to me. I am forever grateful that my husband has always supported me in my decisions. And as the years passed and I leaned into my corporate writing, and spent time with my girls, I was happy. And with my happiness the fearful voices in me grew silent. They mumbled a bit again when I decided to listen even more to My Heart. I was voluntarily saying goodbye to a business with high-level corporate clients that I had been writing for, to start writing more from my Heart. In 2013 I founded my company, Room for Reflection. It came out of a strong desire to help children find joy in life. I had recently ghostwritten a book on students with stress. It makes me so sad to think about children who have had the joy of life stolen from them before they have even really begun to live. When a child is stressed early in life, it affects them in many unforeseen and sometimes tragic ways.

As I looked at my young girls I knew I was doing so many things right. But I also knew that things are different for them because they are growing up in The Digital Age. With society spinning so rapidly it's crucial that we teach our children to listen to their inner voices, and know how they affect us. Consider how much our environment affects the vibrations of our inner voices - so pure and loving in the beginning, but also so easily affected by darkness. If parents or teachers broadcast negative frequencies to children it can create disharmonies in the child and make the child believe that the tunes of life are played in minor. I know from my own life that meditation can help us understand our inner landscapes and listen to the many voices inside of us and especially our hearts. That led me to write "The Children's Meditations in my Heart" that has help thousands of children all over the world turn off their racing thoughts, tune into the love inside of them, and fall asleep naturally.

Today, eleven years after beginning to decipher the recipe of perfect motherhood I now know that there is no such thing. Motherhood comes with so many challenges and I often fail. Perfect motherhood is no longer a goal for me. However, the more I let My Heart guide me in the way I parent, the better it feels for both me and my girls. And by training to listen to My Heart every single day of parenting I train my girls to listen to their hearts as well. This training comes in many ways - from giving myself time and permission to reflect before I parent, remembering to parent myself first and take care of myself, becoming more conscious, analyzing our energy, looking into the many mirrors my daughters hold in front of me, and always do my best to try to the them connect with love.

I now understand that The Voice of my Heart is My Intuition connected to a greater source of universal love through my soul. When I listen to My Heart I have direct access to the wisdom of my soul and can channel from the universe and my guardian angels. As I slowly begin to understand how all of what we call life is so beautifully composed and connected, I feel a strong urge to share my story. I know it is now time for me to rise. If children are taught to see their inner light and listen to the voices, vibrations, and wisdom of their beautiful souls, the world will be lifted and become brighter, and even more magical.

About the Author

Gitte Winter Graugaard, is a Danish writer, life coach, energy mentor, and lightworker. She is on a mission to assist parents in helping their children to thrive through child meditation. Gitte makes parents aware of their energy and what they radiate to their children. She teaches them to always parent themselves first, before they parent their children. Gitte is also the founder of the Momo Academy (www.momo-academy.com), which enables Danish schools to offer mindfulness to their pupils as part of their education. She also coaches parents and provides workshops.

Check out her blog at www.Roomforreflection.com and www.Facebook.com/RoomforReflectionint for the latest news on child meditation and mindfulness.

Sisters Speak Out

Missy Crutchfield

The Perfect Storm

It was a big day for the city department I was leading. After the success of our week-long Gandhi Visits Chattanooga tour in partnership with Mahatma Gandhi's grandson, Arun Gandhi, it was supposed to be the perfect finale to wrap up the events. We had visited the women's economic council annual meeting, the local children's hospital, and then the tour was supposed to culminate with a talk on conflict resolution at the local arts and science magnet school, where my son was a student.

But what had started off as one of the best days of the week quickly became a perfect storm, as I found myself sitting with my son in the principal's office.

While my son and I were waiting for the principal to join us, I spotted a copy of the local newspaper on the coffee table— something I had come to loathe for their political and personal attacks in the Op-Ed section.

I had already been a media "sweetheart" over the last couple of decades. I had returned to Chattanooga after pursuing an acting career in New York and had been lambasted for acting in what the local talk radio station described as a "soft porn" movie. The criticism was so harsh that I finally called the Screen Actors Guild (SAG) to ask about the rating of the film. The SAG representative laughed when I mentioned the term "soft porn" and said, "Missy, what part of the country are you from?" I told them "The South— and we consider Chattanooga the buckle of the Bible belt." They simply responded, "Hmmm, that explains a lot. The film you were in was rated 'R'." Even so, I never heard the end of derogatory remarks in my hometown media for my film roles.

Against my better judgment, I decided to thumb through the newspaper to see what small-town political torpedoes were coming from Drew Johnson's column in the Op-Ed section. I have to mention here that Drew is a conservative pundit who had attacked Al Gore on a regular basis. Now that he had moved to Chattanooga, he decided to focus on me and my family as the subjects for his newest political attack campaign. As I glanced over the pages, I saw it: "Crutchfield comeback? Tennessee Waltz may not have been ex-lawmaker's last turn on the floor."

The glaring headline was followed by yet another ugly attack piece about my father, former Tennessee Senate Majority Leader Ward Crutchfield.

My stomach turned as my mind was quickly flooded by memories of the past five years and my father's arrest during the Tennessee Waltz sting operation that took down several long-time statesmen.

Lately, Drew Johnson had also been attacking the funding of the Education, Arts & Culture department I was administrator of and there were digs about my political family roots and my New York acting career. Having read Drew's distasteful remarks, though, one newspaper reader wrote a letter to the editor saying, "what has this woman done other than act in an 'R' rated movie, that you are pinning a scarlet letter to her chest?" It was a good question.

Of course, no mention was made of the positive impact of my father's public service, his role in the Civil Rights movement, for instance. He brought the first African American onto the floor of the State Legislature to the jeers of his colleagues and told them to "get used to it. And he will be back." Years later, that man, Mr. C.B. Robinson, went on to become a statesman himself, Representative C.B. Robinson.

Suddenly, my attention flashed back to the principal's office as she entered the room. By her demeanor, I sensed this was no ordinary meeting. I listened as she explained what was happening and found myself slammed by a perfect storm.

On that very day, as we wrapped up a successful week-long tour of Gandhi Visits Chattanooga at schools and communities across my hometown, my father was being attacked yet again by the local newspaper and my son was being suspended from school for marijuana possession.

It had been the best of times, and now it was the worst of times. And over the next six months, my life as I knew it would come to a crashing halt.

What Doesn't Kill You Makes You Stronger

My son entered Washington Alternative School, a last stop for minors who have been suspended from school but not sent to juvenile detention.

So here I was, a single mom facing the challenges of raising a very cute, very smart young man with a lot of potential, but he wasn't using his potential for good and he wasn't making good choices. He was acting compulsively and on temptation without considering the consequences. He was failing to realize how his poor decisions were wreaking havoc on his family, friends, community, and himself.

As I reflected back on my own childhood and teen years, I realized that I had faced similar challenges to what my son was going through—I too was different, I too didn't feel like I fit in, I too acted out in my own form of resistance.

In elementary school, I was bullied, which was a frightening experience for a young girl. When I left home and moved to New York at the age of 17 to pursue an acting career, I had just $300 in my pocket and nothing more from my parents. I was looking for the bright lights of the big city—but I was more like a deer caught in the headlights.

A friend recently commented that it was like the "light at the end of the tunnel" turned out to be a freight train.

I modeled for fashion and travel magazines. I held roles in films like Brian de Palma's "Blowout" starring John Travolta and "Carnival Magic." And I held lead roles in "New York Nights" with William DaFoe and "Model Behavior."

I loved the bright lights of New York City, but at the same time, I also experienced the dark side of that world. The sides that the public doesn't see behind those magazine spreads, those movie scenes:

...the models struggling with eating disorders and addictions to fit that "perfect" anorexic image celebrated in the eighties...

...the party scenes with drugs and Playboys and everything else that follows...

...the struggle to get that "big break" taking scripts for "R" rated movies and "B" films...

Celebrities and legends walked into my life from Ruben Blades and Cleveland Amory to Peter Beard, Rick James and Lauren Hutton... and those moments spent with them, their influence, imprinted me for my future life and work.

It was a long journey from New York to public service. As with so many things that have happened in my life, including learning some pretty hard life lessons in New York, I came to learn that what doesn't kill you truly makes you stronger.

My son's own journey toward adulthood has been a long and perilous one since that fateful day when he was first suspended from school. Since then, we have had to change schools for various reasons almost every year.

Following his high school graduation and before he even had a chance to start college, I faced the painful experience no mother ever wants to endure—my son was arrested and spent time in jail on marijuana possession and various other minor and nonviolent charges. This happened not once, but multiple times over the course of the next couple of years. He spent his birthday, Christmas, and even my birthday in jail.

It was heart breaking to watch my child spiral downward into addiction and then have to reap the life-altering consequences. However, when all seems lost, we must continue to remind ourselves that darkness comes before the dawn. In these terrible times, I have often thought of a drawing my son made in elementary school for a suicide prevention event. When I asked him to show me his caricature and tell me about it, he looked up at me and handed me the paper with the drawing and message. It read: "Hell is just the shadow of heaven." I was floored and amazed...

All of these years later, as a family trying to pick up the pieces, I still remember this drawing and my son's description. We have survived our own sort of hell as a family while struggling to deal with the darkness of political turmoil, addiction and incarceration.

Today, I am grateful to say my son has experienced the beginning of transformation—almost like someone flipped a light switch on. This is what I have been praying for: He has awakened to his life's purpose and he is beginning his path of self-transformation. He is also focusing on global change; his passion is turning around environmental devastation and protecting the planet.

As with all things in life, though, my son's transformation is a work in progress. There is still much to be done and much change to come. But that is what life is all about. We never wake up one day and find that we are suddenly perfect. Life is a journey, and we wake up to learn new lessons and make new changes in our lives each day. And, hopefully, we also inspire positive change in the lives of others.

I believe from these experiences that God has prepared me to be on the front line of communicating, reaching out, and trying to inspire women, girls, and all people—starting with my own child, my son—about things that can change your life and positive things that can turn your life around. It's never too late. Every day is a brand-new opportunity to begin your life again, to embrace compassion, to embrace forgiveness, starting with yourself.

When In Hell, Keep Going

My job came to an end with the Mayoral Election, when my boss, the current Mayor, finished his second four-year term and the new Mayor decided to lay off almost the entire cabinet of administrators, including me.

So here I was at the height of my career, or so I thought, having served in leadership positions in media, higher education, and government—mainly male-dominated fields. I had been appointed by the current Mayor Ron Littlefield to establish a City Department of Education, Arts & Culture—a dream job!

From the beginning, we were at the forefront of using the arts and creativity to address social issues in our community, from bullying and gang violence to race relations and economic development. We had been nationally recognized by organizations ranging from the National Education Association to the Arts Education Partnership. Even so, timing is everything. In this case, the timing was off and everything was over.

As the daughter of a political family and head of a department that had "arts" and "culture" in its name, I became the poster child for what the local Tea Party didn't value—the arts, creativity, cultural and civic engagement and literacies, and the intangible way these things impact communities and cities.

So I—like so many others at that time—found myself out of work, and out of a career that spanned a couple of decades of senior leadership in higher education and government, ultimately running a department for a city, and creating that department for the city.

As I well know, though, everything in politics changes. People come and go. Political terms end, elections take place, the new guy comes in with his ideas on things, then one day your time is up and you're left thinking to yourself, "Wow! What am I going to do now?" So many of us define ourselves by our careers, and the end of a job or a career is like experiencing a death. But with every death comes an opportunity for rebirth.

Thinking back, I am reminded of the vision that drove me forward in those eight years leading EAC, through the ups and downs of being a single mom raising a son to enduring ongoing political attacks on my family, friends, and co-workers.

Years ago, I had received a powerful vision in a dream-like state—I was impressed the arts can change the world, and the arts need to be used to address social issues. Shortly after, the newly elected Chattanooga Mayor appointed me founding administrator of the brand-new Department of Education, Arts & Culture (EAC).

Inspired by that original vision I received, "Remember Your Dream" was the driving vision of EAC's initiatives, which included mentoring and arts programs that offered hope and healing to young people who are held back by life's challenges.

Having spent much time working with domestic violence organizations, I was very aware of the devastating effects of DV and child abuse. I met children and adults who had suffered this, who had great potential for their lives but who had become so broken and angry that they had lost sight of love or dreams for their own lives. I realized then that the arts are an instrumental vehicle for healing social issues. The arts had the power to melt broken hearts and open healing and transformation for children who had never experienced love and who had given up on their dreams.

I also had the opportunity to facilitate a Clothesline Project workshop at a women's support group, in which women who have survived domestic violence share their message through t-shirt art. Sometimes a friend or family member will create one for a loved one who has suffered or who is no longer with us... I saw how empowering the t-shirt project was for victims healing and emerging as survivors. I was so moved by their words and images. I began thinking how can we take this to the next level, how can we connect the dots? This stuff is good—how do we bring it to life? That's when I began to think of the spoken word and theater piece "Sisters Speak Out: The Clothesline Speaks." From a full three-act play, workshop sessions, and a documentary, "Sisters Speak Out" has become a project that connects the dots between social issues and the arts in a real and tangible experience from painting t-shirts or quilt squares to hearing the voices of healing and empowerment. It's all about flipping the downward spiral up.

To this day, my social media handle is "SistersSpeakOut" carrying forward that original vision and my continued mission to stand up and speak out for peace and justice not just for women and girls, but for "All God's Children" and for "All God's Creatures."

With a new chapter unfolding in my life, I realized my purpose and passion for social change doesn't die with the end of a job or the end of a project. With deep, soul introspection in the months that followed, I began to see the next iteration of who I am and what I've always wanted to be, and I realized that Gandhi's Be Magazine (www.bemagazine.org), which I co-founded in partnership with my best friend Melissa Turner, was the platform where my work for global change would take the stage.

My Life Is My Message

So, I had to experience all of these things. Ultimately, it helped me feel the deepest connection of empathy and compassion for all people, all cultures, and all living things. I take it all the way to the animals because my first exposure to activism was through the animal rights movement. I believe once your awareness and compassion become heightened, you realize we have to take it beyond human to human. We take it to the planet and all of its inhabitants, and we begin to connect even deeper with our mind, body, spirit, people and planet to heal all and embrace a deeper spirituality as well.

Today I spend a lot of my time sharing with others the realization of our global and planet interconnectivity—between humans, animals and plant life, as our survival truly depends on this amazing web, ecosystem, and interconnectivity of life forms and existence. That's why our most recent work with Gandhi's Be Magazine revolves around Gandhi-inspired stories, posts from around the world, and activism around the Vegan movement, this Vegan Revolution. We've reworked the well-known Gandhi phrase "Be The Change" and turned it into #VTheChange. We call this "the intersection of all intersections" because I believe that once our compassion is heightened, all roads lead to nonviolence— nonviolence to each other, the animals, in our thoughts and in our actions. It's all connected. We are all connected.

We want to (and we need to) take care of each other because of this connectivity, and while we're lifting up this awareness of compassion for one another as "All God's Children" we'll also lift up "All God's Creatures." Everything then falls into place. I'm honored to be part of this movement for global change and nonviolence for all living things, and I'm blessed to be working with so many global change-makers—my brothers and sisters around the world—working on these issues and working to "Be The Change" they wish to see. This is the only way real change will happen. As Gandhi said, "My Life Is My Message." Let our message stand for peace on planet Earth and justice for "All God's Children" and "All God's Creatures" because truly "We Are One."

Be the Change You Wish to See

Now is the time to join this movement for change. I invite you to join us on Gandhi's Be Magazine (www.bemagazine.org) to learn how you can join our growing global community of change-makers around the world who are "being the change" they wish to see. We offer "The Course in Nonviolent Living" and "#VTheChange: A Course in The Vegan Way of Life" to introduce you and empower you in carrying forward Mahatma Gandhi's legacy of nonviolence as a way of living. We are the next generation of Gandhi's, King's, and Mother Teresa's and all the great ones before us who came with messages of peace and love. And as the Hopi Elders say, "We are the ones we have been waiting for."

About the Author

Missy Crutchfield is Co-Founder of Gandhi's Be Magazine and Gandhi Global Center For Peace (which she co-founded with Mahatma Gandhi's grandson Arun Gandhi). She is a globally recognized, award-winning journalist and human rights/animal rights and vegan activist. Missy loves travel, exploring new cultures, spending time with her dogs at home, and cooking vegan. Missy has worked as an actress in NYC and held numerous roles in media. Passionate about addressing social issues through the arts, Missy created and collaborated on a number of projects and community-based programs including "Remember Your Dream," mentoring youth through arts and social issues, and "Sisters Speak Out," an original three-act play and workshop series about domestic violence and women and girl's empowerment.

Through Gandhi's Be Magazine, Missy has covered national and international events, including The Visit of His Holiness the Dalai Lama at Emory University, the 9/11 Unity Walk in Washington, D.C., touring Sean Penn's JP/HRO in Haiti and meeting with Haitian First Lady Sophia Martelly, and covering the travels and speaking engagements of Arun Gandhi.

www.BEMagazine.org

Save ALL LIFE

Siena Pennington

When I was six years old, I was walking with my mom and about to eat an orange. I saw a homeless man on the street and wanted to help him, but all I had with me was that orange. I wasn't that hungry so I gave it to him. Although this was just a tiny act of kindness, it was really my first big step in charity.

A few years later, while living in Italy, we were driving home from school. My mom stopped and invited a lady into our car. This was weird for me because I didn't know this woman or anything about her. Throughout the entire car ride, I tried to understand what she was saying, but I didn't know enough Italian to understand what she was saying. We dropped the woman at her home, she was so happy. I turned to my mom and asked, "Uuuuhhh, what just happened? Why did you invite that lady into our car?"

My mother told me that her husband had recently died, so she didn't have anyone else to drive her home. I had no idea that lady had such a sad story, or that the simple act driving her home would help her so much.

A few years later, my mom caught me frowning in the back seat of the car. She asked me what was wrong, and I told her that I had seen a man on the side of the street. I wanted to help him so much, but I thought that we couldn't pull over to help him. Turns out, I thought right—we couldn't stop to help him at that moment. But, the next morning, when we passed him again, he actually had a whole entourage of friends.

Don't get me wrong; I'm not trying to say don't help the homeless on the off chance that they might actually have a Hollywood-sized entourage of friends. I'm saying that being aware of those in need around you is the first step in finding ways to help.

My mom understood that seeing people living without food and shelter really affected me. From that moment on, we made it a priority to donate our clothes more often. But that wasn't enough for me. I wanted to know the people that I was donating to. I really wanted to be part of it—at least, more than I was then.

I was completely overwhelmed, so I asked my mom what I could possibly do. I was just a little eight-year-old trying to save lives. She told me that I had to start small and grow step by step until I was big. So, I did. And my first step was to create a donation bucket. I filled the bucket with my allowance to donate to a charity.

Another one of my outlets for helping others was veganism. I want to help save all lives, not just humans. When I was seven years old, I went vegetarian. My compassion for animals was why I made the step, but I had no idea at that time how important it was. I educated myself even further and went fully vegan for my love of animals! I learned that animals are not only mistreated and killed in the meat industry, but also that they are held in inhumane conditions solely to provide eggs and milk for human consumption. So, when I was ten years old, I went **vegan.** And I am so happy I did!

Earlier this year, while at a sleepover with my friend, we decided to start a charity. We hung up posters in our town to raise money to help the local homeless. We have also started an Etsy shop online where we are selling 100% recycled, handmade accessories. _All_ profit goes to charity. I'm so happy to finally have an outlet for both my creativity and my passion for helping others!

Now I want to go global and have an even bigger impact. My mission for Save All Life is to give back to as many lives as possible. To do that, I need _your_ help to _save all life._ To **donate,** please visit www.SaveAll.Life

About the Author

Siena Pennington is a change maker from the next generation. At the age of 11, she has already started her own charity to *Save All Life*.

For more information go to www.SaveAll.Life

TIME TO RISE

2

LIFE REDEFINED

No Regrets

Deri Llewellyn-Davies

"It's time to rise…"

I love that phrase! The moment that Andrea reached out and asked me if I would be a part of this message, I just said, "yes—count me in."

So, what's my story…? *What did I rise up for?*

I stand for two things: business and life. My core message throughout everything I do is to 'live a life of no regrets, and build a business (or career) of no regrets.' Easily said, but not so easy to do.

So, let's address both together. But firstly, let me ask you a question…

If you died today, would you go out with any regrets? Would you be fulfilled, going out knowing that you had fully lived?

That's a difficult question to ask yourself, I know.

Twelve years ago, I posed that question to myself at a pivotal point in my life.

And honestly, I didn't like the answer I got.

I sat on my father's hospital bed and looked him in the eye. He left his legacy for me by giving me the one phrase that would change my life forever. The one phrase I live by today, and the one phrase I would die by—I very nearly have once already!

But first, let me introduce myself and give you some context. My name is Deri Llewellyn-Davies, and in the business world, I'm known as 'The Strategy Man. I have been blessed to have an amazing business career spanning two decades, but it has only been

70

in the last twelve years, since this pivotal moment with my father, that I have found genuine fulfillment.

I have been operating at European board level for billion-dollar corporations, run no less than twenty of my own businesses, advised over three hundred other businesses at board level, and I've spoken to thousands around the world. But don't be dazzled by that. The first decade of so-called success felt empty.

I've learned the hard way what is more important to me. What makes me feel alive is living a life of great adventure. Since discovering this about myself, I've climbed six of the highest mountains in the world, completed an Ironman competition, and ran the Marathon des Sables.

I also love being a father to my three beautiful girls, truly being present with them, traveling the world, speaking internationally, making my home in an area of outstanding natural beauty, and creating a life that I'm truly proud of.

Today, I can honestly say that I'm living without regrets. But it wasn't always like this.

I grew up feeling like I didn't fit in. I was adopted, and there was always that sense that I didn't really know who I was. However, I was driven and determined to succeed, and ready to prove myself.

And I did succeed in business. It was a superficial, external kind of success, and it destroyed my soul and left me feeling empty. The bottom line was that no matter what I achieved, nothing would fill that gap.

Do you know the gap I am talking about? I think we all experience a longing for something more meaningful at times.

I dreamed that someday I would be happy, and that if I 'succeeded' enough, then my gap would be filled. I burnt myself out three times on that futile quest.

The road to success was a struggle. Even when I had financial success, I wasn't happy because there was always something more to pursue.

To succeed, I threw myself into professional development very early. And from there, I moved onto an in-depth study of personal development for years. So if you've read all the personal development books out there, and been to seminars and hoping some guru would point the way to bliss, I know how you feel. Because after trying all of that and still feeling like crap, I was ready to give up.

That's when I found myself sitting on my Dad's hospital bed....

My father was a good man and a great influence in my life. To see him die so suddenly through cancer was heartbreaking. But what hurt the most was the legacy he left me.

In his last days, I held his hand on his deathbed, and he looked me deeply in the eye with a look of great sadness. Now, this in its own right was a miracle, as my dad had shown no emotion in his entire life. He was what I would class as "emotionally stunted."

He said, "Deri, I've been such a fool. I wish I'd had the balls to do so much more in life. And to live it fully."

He went on to tell me in great detail about the business opportunity that had slipped through his fingers. He even spoke, rather fondly, of his dream to own a ride-on lawnmower.

So, my father died with his dreams intact. I swore I wouldn't go out that way.

I was not going to be on my deathbed, lying there with regrets. No f**king way. At that point in my life, if I had gone out, I would have had the same regrets as my father. And so, I went to work.

Choosing to go all in and live a life of no regrets is not an easy path to choose. It means that some points in life will be tough. You will have to make the tough decisions, face many fears, and deal with multiple failures along the way. But to not do so is also a choice, and although life itself may seem easier, I promise you that's delusion talking. Taking the easy way, you will still face tough decisions, like fear and failure, but you're just storing it up, putting it off, like my father did. Then he was dealt that devastating blow of realization on the way out.

So, I went deeper to truly know myself. The more work I did on this, the more I knew there was something missing in my soul. That was where my aforementioned gap was.

The big trigger for me was an exercise I completed over ten years ago now. I imagined a future version of me with my grandchildren sitting on my knee, and what I would say to them...

I was imagining something like this.

"Hey, little Bobby. Let Grandpa tell you all about the business deals he was doing in his thirties. Look at this property I bought over here, and look at this over here..."

And little Bobby would have gone to sleep in my lap, bored shitless. Hell, I was boring myself! Where was the adventure, the courage, or the inspiration?

Do you want to try it with me now?

Have a think about your own future self. Who will you be if you carry on down the path you are on now? In your mind's eye, fast-forward 10, 20, 30 years from today.

Your grandkids are sitting on your knee. What story are you telling them?

I had two grandfathers. One fought in the war in North Africa. He used to sit me on his knee and tell me his stories. I was proud of him and he inspired me. The other granddad didn't have much to tell, so I wasn't regaled with tales of his adventures, as there really weren't any.

Remembering that comparison during this exercise really hit me hard. I had nothing to say either—but that wasn't the granddad I wanted to be!

The missing part became clear to me. It was adventure that I wanted—this was the missing piece to fill my inner gap.

At that point in my life, I decided, 'screw it'. If I'm going to go for adventure, then I'm going to go big. I wanted to experience the best this world has to offer and to really explore the globe, living full out.

That to me was the seven highest mountains in the world on every continent, the two poles, the Sahara Desert, the jungle, and an ironman thrown into the mix—I don't know why I chose that one! This was the beginning of what I called: 'The Global Adventurer's Grand Slam.'

No one had quite done it before in that context, so I was going for a bit of a world first on that level. And that's where the journey began. It was just a mere dream and a bit of a crazy idea, and through sheer will, it became a reality.

Now, ten years on, I am proud to say I have the Marathon des Sables, an Ironman, and six summits under my belt. This all cumulated in May of 2015 with my Everest expedition.

The earth moved under my feet

I took a very memorable 'selfie' right on the spine of the ridge of Mount Everest, just before the earthquake actually hit. This is where a bit of luck came in to save me. I had stopped on top of the ridge and had just taken my pack off. As I dropped my pack, it moved to one side, then mysteriously moved back. At that point, **I thought I had gone mental. Was this the altitude messing with my head?**

The next thing I knew, I was riding a bucking bull. But the bull was a rock. I'm serious—at no point did we recognize we were in an earthquake because that is just not heard of on Mt. Everest. It's funny how the mind can't work out what's happening when you are in the middle of things, because the biggest fear you have on any mountain is an avalanche.

In an avalanche you first hear something like thunder, and then you shit yourself! But in this case, there was no thunder; it was just my pack moving without explanation. I lay flat on the ground and held onto the rock for fear I would be thrown off the mountain; it was that severe! But I still did not know what was going on. I still thought I had altitude sickness and was going mad!

Sat Baines, the British Chef, had gone back down Everest two days before. He had HAPE, High Altitude Pulmonary Edema, which is swelling of the lungs, and so he was removed from the mountain. We had already lost four other people to HAPE, and I saw how mental they went. So now that I was 'seeing things,' I thought, "Oh my God, it's me, I've gone mental and the whole world is moving!"

At what point would you think, "Oh I know, this is an earthquake"? The last time an earthquake occurred here was 120 years ago. And back then, no one was daft enough to be climbing Everest! So, we didn't know what we were in.

It lasted about one minute, and it was the longest minute of my life.

I still didn't know what I was experiencing. I was positioned in between two teams as I had gone out on my own. I was still thinking, "Oh my God, I have gone mental," just trying to process what I had just experienced. I was too far away from the others to ask them what it was.

When the Earthquake stopped, there was an eerie silence—then the thunder began. Avalanches started to come down both sides of the valley.

It's a bizarre sound. Imagine the noise of pool balls being released from inside the pool table. Now imagine you are in the middle of the pool machine itself and those balls are moving fast.

Now keep in mind that we are surrounded by the valley. The earthquakes and thunder were happening all around, so after it unleashed avalanches, the mountain shook like it had never been shaken before! Then the ice pinnacles also started to crack. I just sat there, and I swear, I was sat in the palm of God. I'd witnessed Armageddon all around me, but it was a beautiful moment. A surreal, life-changing, PIVOTAL moment.

What happened next is where the power lies. Still in the palm of God, I had a flashback to twelve years before, to where this story began.

So, standing on the north col of Everest, having looked death squarely in the eye… again, I could look back on the past decade and ask myself the big question again.

If I had died on Everest, would I have gone out with regrets?

I was living my life and pursuing adventure, so no, there were no regrets.

But I'm far from over, and I'm here to help people rise up, build businesses that make them proud, and to architect their own lives of no regrets.

And it's also time for me to rise up again. I feel as thought I've only just begun on this journey and there are more adventures to be had! So life's great adventure continues.

About the Author

Deri Llewellyn-Davies is an internationally acclaimed speaker, author, adventurer and entrepreneur who is transforming lives around the world with his core message of *No Regrets*. With a commitment to helping others architect a life and business of *No Regrets*, he passionately and candidly delivers insights from his vast experience in business and adventures in life.

One of the truly unique aspects of his speeches comes from his love of adventure. As he shares in his first book, *Life's Great Adventure*, Deri has climbed five of the highest mountains in the world, run the Marathon des Sables, and completed an IronMan competition.

He also lived to tell his tale of *No Regrets* after surviving the devastating earthquake while climbing Everest in the spring of 2015, which he shared in his hugely popular TEDx presentation.

Learn how to architect your own epic adventure using Deri's Diamond Life Design system. Visit
www.DiamondLifeDesign.com

And for more on creating a business of no regrets, visit
www.BGIStrategy.com

A Letter to My Younger Self

Yvette Taylor

My darling Yvette,

I wanted to take the time to write you a letter, to share what I know now, but didn't know when I was younger. Right now you are eleven years old. For me to describe all the amazing things to come in your life I need to take you back in time because your story starts before you were even born. I know you're going through a tough time. You're wondering what this life is all about. You've got questions. You're angry. You feel unloved and let down. Up to now, life hasn't been kind to you. My wish is for you to understand why this had to happen to you. Because of it you became the person you needed to be.

You come from a family of strong powerful women. They are able to always get back on their feet, no matter how many times they are knocked down. This pattern goes back through the generations. Let's just start with your mum's mum. Nana was born into a wealthy family in Jamaica, where she met Grandad. They fell in love and had two girls, Mum and her sister. Grandad left Jamaica for the UK to create a better life. Over the years they grew apart and separated and their daughters were ferried between the two sides of the family.

Everyone wanted them because Grandad was giving them financial support. But no one really cared about the girls, only the money that came with them. That family was cruel and violent. All Mum felt was loss, heartache, and abandonment.

When she was seven, Mum was beaten by her uncle and left for dead in a ditch because she didn't come home for dinner on time. As she recovered in bed from her injuries, she heard the bus trundle into the village and toot its horn. A few minutes later there was a knock on the door. When Mum opened her eyes Nana walked in. She'd come immediately when she heard what had happened to her little girl. She packed up her two daughters and took them home to safety.

When Mum was about the same age as you are now, Nana was sick in hospital. Grandad sent his family to take Mum and her sister to England. Mum was inconsolable. Nothing could replace the gaping loss of her mum and leaving home.

Mum grew up in England and had four children, two boys and two girls. Those two girls were you and your sister. Sadly Dad was another cruel and unloving man. Though he earned a good wage, he kept most of it to himself. Every week he gave Mum less than £20 to buy food for the family while he went out and drank in the pub.

Mum loved you more than you know. She worked long hours as a dinner lady and cleaner at school to make ends meet. This is why "play time" was spent wandering the empty corridors of the school, or helping to scrub the floors and toilets before you went home.

You hated the fact she was never there, that you didn't have friends to play with and no one was there after school. Sadly, being home didn't feel any better. You were constantly on edge, wondering if Dad would come home drunk and belligerent. A good day for you and your sister, was when you played in your room and stayed out of the way. But there many bad days.

I know the pain you felt as you cowered behind the bedroom door. Or when you hid in the darkness of the wardrobe, your fingers white from gripping the doorknob, as tears slid down your face. Listening to Mum scream, and dad shout. You were eaten up by the guilt of leaving her to protect you because you didn't eat all of your dinner or finish your homework on time.

In a way you were lucky, Yvette. Your older sister protected you and took the brunt of Dad's anger. But too many times you both went to school with black eyes, bumps, and bruises. Knowing there would be no help because the police would shrug it off as a "family matter." I know how many times you dreamt of smothering him with a pillow, or stabbing him in the back. Just to make it stop.

But that wasn't the worst of it. You missed weeks and months of school as you bounced from hospital to home. I remember too well the look of despair on Mum's face as the doctors turned her away, saying your weight gain was normal. Mum knew better. You were not well. Sometimes your eyes were so swollen you could barely open them. Mum was right; your body was shutting down. You had a rare condition known as nephrotic syndrome and your kidneys were failing. You were less than 24 hours from death.

For years the doctors were baffled. They decided to try a cancer treatment before putting you on dialysis for life. You battle the side effects. Things little girls should never have to go through. You lose your thick curly hair, and it will grow in thin and patchy. You swell up and hate seeing your pudgy face in the mirror. The doctor tells you the medication will make you infertile. While this may not bother you now, as you get older, the pain will grow. The hospital becomes your second home. Oh, how you cried for Mum, but Dad wouldn't bring her. You felt so lost and alone.

Years later, after many treatments you get better. You become a teenager and make friends. One Saturday night you tell Mum you're at a friends for a sleepover. What you don't say is that her parents are away and her older sister is having a party.

At the end of the night you are lying on the bathroom floor, the room spinning from too much vodka. There is a boy on top you and you're in excruciating pain as your blood spills on the bathroom carpet and your innocence is taken. When it's over you tell your friend what happened. She doesn't believe you. You tell her sister. She doesn't believe you either. The next morning you get up stiff and sore, and stuff tissues in your knickers so you can walk home. You don't dare to tell Mum because you're scared of your Dad. You decide to keep quiet.

Six weeks later you go to Jamaica for the first time to see your family. You become best friends with your cousin who is three years older than you. She takes you to play down by the river. On the way back you stop at a rundown shack to see her "friend." She goes into the bedroom and closes the door. Her "friend's" friend sits next to you on the sofa. He starts to kiss you. You can't stop him, he is much stronger, and he has a knife. All you can do is lie still and wait for it to be over.

Again, you decide to keep it to yourself.

Back in England a few months later. You have this deep, sad, pain in your heart. You're angry and you don't know why.

It happens again. This time it's your babysitter's brother. You've known him all your life. He invites you round to roll a joint in his bedroom. You don't fight because you believe this is the way things are. Instead you lie back on the bed, watching the spliff burn away in the ashtray, waiting for it to be over.

Again you keep your silence. You keep this pain bottled up for years. You think you're unworthy, an "object" that men can do whatever they want to. To dull the pain you drink, do drugs, and party. Being numb is better than feeling the darkness of a childhood lost.

At seventeen you do discover something powerful, something that will change your life. You discover energy and you study every book, and take courses and workshops on it.

Why did I begin this letter with Mum? Because these things didn't only happen to you. What I now understand is that patterns are passed down through the generations, from both sides of the family. Whether you call it DNA or family genetics, it is ALL just energy.

Even though you weren't even yet born, everything that happened to Mum—and to her mum and to her mum—is imprinted in you. Like so many others, our family is built on loss, pain, violence, abuse, and abandonment. You came into this life carrying it. It is your soul's journey to break those patterns for everyone—past, present, and future.

Your dad will never be the man you wished for. In spite of it all, he didn't know better. He did the best with what he knew. On a soul level, you all agreed to play this story out together. He has deep regrets for his actions. When you turn twenty-nine he'll say, for the first time, three little words; "I love you."

Your illness was your body's way of protecting you, to get you out of a situation you didn't want to be in. All those years of abuse had taken its toll. This may not make sense to you now, but in Chinese philosophy your kidneys are the seat of fear. Spending so much time in hospital actually kept you safe.

Remember that no matter WHAT happened to you, it wasn't your fault. It wasn't okay. You were young, you didn't know any better, and you were taken advantage of. That doesn't mean you should put the blame on them. It just is as it was. But know, you did NOT have to suffer alone. Your mum and sister loved you more than you know and would've done anything to protect you.

Know that there will be kind and gentle men in your life. You WILL find a man who loves and adores you. His name is Ade. He will stand by you know matter what. He will be everything you wished for when you were young. He is loving and kind, thoughtful and caring. Together you prove the doctors were wrong in 2014, when they said you could never have children. Ade will be the amazing dad you always wanted to your son Kye.

I know now that you had to experience the suffering and setbacks of your childhood, to become the woman you are today. Without that pain you would never have started your journey of self-discovery.

This was your journey because you ARE strong enough Yvette.

You ARE amazing.

You ARE powerful.

You ARE beautiful.

You always have been and you always will be.

Even though you are only eleven years old, I am everything today, because of who you were then. It was YOU who made me strong.

I want to thank you for the courage, the strength and determination you showed even in the face of your greatest fears.

I want to thank you for never giving up even when life felt so hard and you felt like no one was there to support you.

I want to thank you for the love you showed to others even when you felt like you were dying inside.

You taught me to stay strong and to find friendship.

You taught me to be kind and to love others.

You taught me to forgive and to let go.

You taught me to be keep on going until I found happiness.

These are the lessons you taught me so I could be the woman I am today.

You have no idea how happy your life will be, or how many lives you changed for the better.

Because of you, I'm lucky enough to spend my time changing people's lives as a transformational mentor who helps people let go of resistant energy, thoughts, and emotions to live a life more in flow; a life filled with happiness, love, and a sense of freedom. I never dreamt that I would grow up to be a coach, mentor, or guide (and even have to pinch myself now). At eleven you don't think you have anything to share with the world. Everything that happened feels now like it was another lifetime. But know that together we will touch the lives of millions of men and women around the world.

I am so proud of you. Of everything you've become. ALL that I have accomplished is because of one amazing little girl who wouldn't give up.

To anyone else reading my story, know you are not alone.

All the pain and disappointment of the past hurt you. I know.

But they made you exactly the person you are today.

And what a wonder you are.

If you found your way here, to the amazing stories in this book; you made that happen.

No matter what happens in your life, YOU have the power to rewrite your story. Every day is a chance to start again. Your life is yours. No one else's.

The only thing that ever stands in the way of what you want, is what you think and what you feel. You create change.

I know that now.

It took me a long time to really live it.

And I can't tell you how magical it feels and how far away it seems from the childhood and life I had before.

I don't need drink or drugs to feel like that.

I don't need love or admiration from anyone except me

I don't need to expect anything from anyone.

It is up to ME to make my life happy, ONLY I can do it and it's the same for you too.

But if you want to change your life, you must first claim it.

It ALL begins with changing your energy, thoughts, and emotions.

When you master that your amazing life will unfold.

About the Author

Yvette Taylor is the Creator of EAM—The Energy Alignment Method. This technique has been dubbed "the fastest transformational energy tool for getting in flow," by Hay House Author, Jo Westwood. Yvette has spent seventeen years studying, teaching and sharing energy and spiritual principles. She is on a mission to touch the lives of millions to help them feel more empowered, in flow, and to help them change their lives. She was Voted the Top 10 Holistic Therapist In The UK – Holistic Therapy Magazine and Winner Platinum Award for best therapist and practice 2017. Yvette is an entrepreneur and change maker at heart, who has taken not one but two companies from zero to six and seven figures in less than eighteen months.

If you're ready to discover how to stay in flow and change your life with energy, check out www.energyalignmentmethod.com

The Art of Not Figuring it Out

Katrine Sunniva Spiegelhauer

I always knew how to figure it out. For as long as I can remember, I always found a way to know what was expected of me.

February 2003

My firstborn. A boy. Only a few hours old. Curly ginger hair and my own sparkling blue eyes stared back at me. His perfect little round face with rosy cheeks and an intense look reflected an old man's wisdom. As I looked into his eyes I felt...failure. I should have felt happiness, love, gratitude, fulfillment, or other "motherly" feelings. I should have felt anything but this. Instead I felt like a failure, and then I felt wrong for feeling like a failure.

I couldn't figure it out. I looked around in the semidarkness of the sterile hospital room, searching for someone, anyone, who could help me. But I was alone. I looked back at my son, who was still staring intensely at my face, as if he was trying to tell me something. It was like he could *see* me; as if he understood the turmoil inside of me. "I'm sorry," I whispered. What is expected of me? Certainly not this.

The birth was a "normal" hospital birth after Danish standards. The midwife was busy and young, and I didn't like the way she spoke to me. So I turned my back to her and told her to leave me alone. That was not a "nice" thing to do. I prefer to be nice to people but am not always successful. I also wanted a natural birth, so I when I finally accepted the epidural, I felt like I was betraying myself, betraying my son. I'd failed. At least that's how I felt. It was a familiar feeling, so I believed it was true. I gave my son my breast. He suckled and closed his eyes, and I felt a little better. This I can do. Feeding your child is a motherly thing to do.

So I figured it out as I always do. I went shopping with my mum for organic clothes, mattress, diapers, you name it. I power yoga-ed the extra pounds off. The baby and I listened to classical music, he started baby swim classes, and I sang to him to stimulate his nervous system and his brain development. I *can do this*, I thought. After all, I'm a psychologist specializing in perinatal mental health.

He was a happy child. Always smiling. When he wasn't crying, that is. When he'd cry I would feed him. He cried. I would feed him some more. I was exhausted. He grew plumb and round. On his little narrow shoulders he carried the burden of making me the perfect mum. It all looked good, on the surface, but behind my high achieving, perfect mum image, I felt like a failure. I felt like a fraud—lost, and alone. The strategy that had worked all my life—figure it out, and do what is expected—was not enough for motherhood.

I should have learned my lesson three years earlier.

Shame is Subtle

In 2000 my love and I went to Kerala, in Southern India, to celebrate a new millennium; a time full of promise. We'd gone through some tough times. Trying for a baby can be really hard on a relationship. When we came back to Denmark and I was were still not pregnant, I asked him to see a doctor. Within an hour he called me. The doctor told him to get a CT scan immediately, and that he'd need an operation within the week. A few days later, as we went to the hospital to get the results, he said, "if I have to go through chemotherapy, we're getting married." I said yes. But it didn't seem like a celebration.

The results showed a very rare sarcoma. The doctor had to call his colleagues in the UK. My love was sitting pale-faced, his eyes blank. *We're going to get married*, I thought. But there were no fluttering butterflies in my stomach, no joy, only despair, pain, and shame.

Shame is subtle—it works its way into your subconscious through your experiences, and associations. The love of my life was diagnosed with cancer and my primary emotion was shame. Like it was somehow my fault. Shame popped up, looked at me hard and said, "look what you've done, shame on you!"

While, my love, was in hospital listening to the nauseating drip-dripping of the poison flowing into his veins I sat on the floor of our living room, with all the pieces of my life and identity scattered around me, trying to solve the puzzle of my shame. What did I miss? When did I lose control over my life? The answer was mocking and very familiar: You are not in control. Who do you think you are? You are selfish, arrogant and narcissistic. THAT is why things are falling apart. I knew that voice. The voice of my Inner Self Critic, the lifetime partner of my old friend, Shame. I knew them well. Perhaps if I'd stopped for a moment and listened I would've saved myself a lot of pain, frustration, and exhaustion. Perhaps if the voice was the gentle whisper of Compassion and not the loud blast of Shame, I might have. But I was going to prove it wrong. I was going to FIGURE THIS OUT! Because that's what I know how to do. Or so I thought.

2007

It was not until when I was about to give birth to our second child, a daughter, that I got a vague sense of what I had totally missed when I gave birth to my son. I was exhausted. I could not keep up with figuring it all out. I'd realized that always striving for perfection made me a less than perfect mum and it definitely didn't make me happy. I had to stop trying to figure out what was expected of me but I needed more than that. I needed a village around me. I needed women who made me feel safe, and most important and also the most difficult for me: I had to let go of achieving. I had to surrender to whatever would be.

Easier said than done.

After I gave birth to my daughter, I looked at her, deeply. In the same way I'd looked at my son when he arrived four years earlier. She looked back. I felt curiosity, I felt joy, I felt strong, I felt a disturbing sense of responsibility, but I didn't feel failure. The Inner Self Critic was unusually quiet. I *had* figured somethings out.

The following months we sold the house and went to India and Nepal. We traveled for eight months with a four year old and a three-month-old baby. Not everybody was happy for me. The voice of Shame was muffled, but Others, whose opinion mattered to me, showed their discontent. But for once Defiance was louder than Shame.

Under the Indian sky, a new calm and joyful version of me was unfolding. Away from the disapproving glances of Others, we flourished. For the first time in my life I felt the freedom of not having to figure out what was expected of me. That said, being a mother and a psychologist I could always hear the 'shoulds' *and* the 'oughts' that would feed my Inner Critic.

My husband had been on a journey to rediscover his body after the chemotherapy and had spend the past two years becoming a yoga teacher and we continued the journey together. We would roll out the mats every morning before the heat was too strong and we would sit together breathing, becoming one with all. Everything made sense without me trying to make sense of it. No one expected anything from me, and if they did, I didn't try to figure it out. Instead I listened, to my children, to my body, to my love. Every night I would sit watching the sunset as hundreds of butterflies fluttered around me into the sky. *Life can be like this*, I thought, as I sat there, filled with Gratitude. My Inner Critic was silent. I was learning to listen and to let go. However, things would get much worse before they got better.

2012

I was back in Denmark, driving through the woods on my way to a meeting. The feeling of contentment I'd found in India was long gone, replaced by work and daily life. I was running late, visualizing an available parking spot in front of the entrance. It was spring. A soft green light surrounded me, as the road curved through the trees. I was going too fast and decided to slow down. But nothing happened. "Lift your foot" I said, but couldn't. I felt paralyzed. A sharp turn ahead was getting closer. I was still going too fast, and I couldn't get my brain to tell my foot to press the break. A car was coming toward me, but my body still didn't respond. I saw a large oak tree ahead of me. *If I drive into that tree, I will at least stop*, I thought. I saw my bed before my eyes, sensed the clean crisp linen and the familiar smells of home. I wanted only to lay my head down on my pillow and close my eyes. Just for a while. My breath slowed down, my muscles relaxed. I lifted my foot, stepped on the brake and turned the car to the side of the road.

I sat there for a while, embraced by the lush green light. I felt cracked open.

I drove home and went straight to bed and stayed there staring at the wall for three weeks. I wasn't alone. Shame and my Inner Critic joined me.

Those three weeks are a blur to me. I don't remember eating or going to the bathroom. Plates of food and cups of tea appeared on the bedside table then disappeared again. Every day my children would come to me and give me a cuddle or show me a drawing. I tried to smile, but my face was numb. Selma, our third child, was only two years old. She would tiptoe quietly into the bedroom, sneak into the bed, curl up next to me, and it would break my heart. I felt her soft cheeks, her tiny fingers wrapped around mine. I took in the scent of her hair, and the sound of her sleeping breath, and tried to come back to her, back to a world outside of myself but couldn't. Shame reared her ugly face and shook her head. I agreed. I was the lousiest mother in the world.

Onward

Thus began a slow and painful journey back to life. I eventually went back to work but what had once seemed like a fantastic opportunity to support mothers and children through tough circumstances was now a constant confirmation that I was simply putting out fires. I was clearly an example. I quit my job to once again try to figure it out. The Inner Critic and Shame were having a ball, one louder than the other. They didn't even pause to sleep at night. I had their constant chatter in my ears 24/7. They were even with me on my yoga mat. I had no safe place.

And there was that crack in me. It was still there from when I'd fought not to drive off the road. As Leonard Cohen says: "cracks are where the light gets in." With the light came Defiance and Compassion.

Let me introduce you to Compassion. She is always there. Lingering in the background, whispering in her soft voice. She carries the burden of the suffering of the world on her strong shoulders. She knows suffering and has the wisdom and dedication to alleviate it. But you must acknowledge her. To me, Compassion was always directed outward, toward Others. Shame had taught me that Compassion was not for me. I could not ask for it, I could not receive it from Others, and I most definitely could not show it toward myself. Compassion for myself would be self-indulgent, narcissistic, and would take Compassion away from someone who needed or deserved it more. Shame had always been clear about this.

But through the crack I could hear the whispers of Compassion. I realized that Compassion is not only for Others, and can't grow from always figuring-out-what-is-expected. Compassion sits by your bedside in your darkest hours, whispering to you. It grows like the lotus flower through the mud toward the light. She is there through all your losses, your insecurities, your anger and resentment, your suffering and your shame. And when she breaks the surface, through the mud toward the light, or through the crack in your armor, she sheds her light on everything, even you.

Not long after, I started my own business as a narrative therapist working with mothers and helping them through their stories of pregnancy, birth, motherhood and loss. And I began to work the muscle of Compassion, not only toward them but toward myself. As the saying goes, depression hates a moving target.

Shame is always with me—like an itch on my back that I just can't reach—but so is Compassion. When I listen to her and hold her in my mind and body, I can reach out beyond Fear and fight for for all the other mothers out there, who are battling in the arenas of Shame, Guilt, Perfection, and Figuring-it-Out.

I know now that everything I have been through, the last fifteen years, has prepared me for this. Would I like to have known this sooner? Do I wish I'd listened more? Yes but I am no longer in the business of beating myself up.

A post on Instagram read: Everything is figureoutable. But it isn't. Sometimes you can't figure it out. Like motherhood, sometimes you have to let go and surrender to the wisdom of Compassion.

About the Author

Katrine Sunniva Spiegelhauer is Clinical Psychologist, Mentor, and a Storyworker. An authorized clinical psychologist, she has specialized in perinatal mental health. She has many years experience of listening to mothers. As a narrative therapist Katrine has worked with stories of pregnancy, birth, motherhood and loss and has trained and supervised professionals in the perinatal field. She is also a mother of three. She gathers groups of women with a shared passion for empowering mothers and has developed the Compassion Focused Mother Care Program.

Mission Possible

Susana Mei Silverhøj

Sanna, time has come. You are ready for your mission.

I have always been a seeker. I've always known that I am on a BIG mission. That I am here to make a difference in the world. Although, one of my greatest frustrations in life has been that I didn't know *what* that mission was. So I kept on searching around the world, through education and relationships, and within. I acted on my visions, intuitions, and inner "knowing," even if I never understood where they would lead me.

I never liked kids. I did not see myself ever working with children. But I always wanted to work for them. My heart would ache when children suffered or were hurt. Knowing that I never liked children, you might question why I wanted to have children of my own. For me, it was simply a knowing. I knew I was going have three or even four children. It was never a matter of choice or something to question. It was a knowing from my heart. I even knew the moment I was going to be pregnant. On July 4th, 2003, my inner voice said: "If you want to get pregnant. This is the time." I was, on the couch reading and wasn't even thinking about sex. No! I don't want to get pregnant now. I could feel my heart beating hard and fast at just the thought. I wasn't sure I was ready at all. I should finish my master's degree in developmental psychology first. *Damn you voice!* I thought.

Then I heard myself call out for my husband.

The moment our daughter arrived, I knew life would never be the same.

Years came and went as I searched, trying to find out what was my mission. We had a second child, and I became deeply depressed. I lost all faith and willingness to live. My children were the only reason I stayed. I slowly started to rise from the darkness of those years. Then I had a miscarriage. Another descent into darkness. We had a third child. Oh, such joy. But, that pregnancy activated fibromyalgia. I was in constant pain 24/7 for over a year. I woke up every morning crying.

Our son was in first grade, when I was in chronic pain from fibromyalgia. Our children were all at a private Waldorf school or day care in Denmark, since their pedagogical values were aligned with ours. Or so we thought. With over thirty children in one class our son was not getting the individual attention he needed and he started to act out. We didn't understand what was happening to our happy, loving boy, but I knew intuitively that his openness and sensitivity made him susceptible to everyone's energies and to their blocked and suppressed emotions. We went to a holistic practitioner, recommended by the school, who told us that it was a physical imbalance between his heart and lungs; from complications he had at birth. We were relieved. He would take some homeopathic medicine to support and balance his body.

A few days later, at a meeting with his teacher, we tried to explain the doctor's diagnosis. She interrupted us and asked, "Do you hit your children, because there has to be a reason why he is acting this way?" We were stunned. How could we find a solution and support our son and change this behavior if his own teacher saw him and us as the problem? Was that the only explanation she could come up with, that we abuse our children? And the school backed up her point of view. We felt so powerless and helpless. Were we bad parents? Were we not good enough? Were we not doing enough?

A few days later we were offered a dream job, running a hotel in Costa Rica. It had been one of my visions and dreams for over twenty years. Finally it felt that the universe was working with us. Everything was leading up to this. It started to make sense why this happened at school with our son. There was a lot of resistance, from family and our daughter, to so abruptly change our life. We didn't have a lot of money make the move, didn't speak Spanish very well, and had no school yet for the kids. But we had to follow our heart.

In Costa Rica, we hired a private tutor to teach our children Spanish, and I found my teacher, mentor, and friend, Tup, a shaman. He helped me turn my life around. His teaching helped reduce my fibromyalgia symptoms and I felt whole again. The more I understood who I am, why I am here—my history, ancestry, legacy and my soul's journey—the more worthy and "me" I felt. I started to enjoy life again. I felt at peace, like I was on the right track. I was ready to go back to Denmark. Confident that now life would be amazing.

Coming back was a shock for all of us. The dense energy in the northern countries, the stress of perfectionism; the impossible task to do everything society tells us to do, *perfectly*. I calculated how many hours we would need to clean, cook, work full time, exercise, sleep, have a social life, nurture your children, and husband, and have hobbies. Turns out we need *eleven* days a week. In that calculation there is no time for self-nurturing at all. That was the life we came back to.

It wasn't all bad, our sons were happy. Our oldest son started at a new school with a very small class of only ten students and quickly made friends. But our daughter was struggling. School was difficult because her friends had formed new friendships and social dynamics while she was away. Her teacher was worried and expressed concerns *that we seemed to put the family's needs before our daughter's.*

I didn't understand this. Should her needs be more important than the whole family's? What kind of family would that be? After many attempts to fit into and do what the school requested we declared ourselves once again defeated. The school had decided that there was something seriously wrong with our family, and we could not convince them otherwise. We once again took the oldest and youngest children out of school.

A longing to have our children experience the world instead of reading about it, grew stronger and stronger. I came up with the "Flow Schooling" concept—a holistic education for a new generation. We left Denmark and traveled through southern Europe for fourteen weeks, exploring different cultures, history, religions, languages, and landscapes.

We were all excited and happy. This was life! Then came the next setback. A few weeks into our tour we received a letter from the municipality. They wanted us to come to a meeting since the Waldorf school had sent in a complaint about us as parents. I was devastated. I started to question myself. Are they right? Are we bad parents? All that we want is to give our children the best foundation in life; to be happy, and live fully with purpose. Could we be wrong? But it was so evident that we had become closer as a family. There were less fights and conflict. We'd all blossomed. How could we be wrong? How could we be bad parents?

We returned to Denmark but my husband and I wanted to keep this new lifestyle. We loved the freedom. We could work remotely from anywhere in the world with our business, so why not? The main challenges were that our daughter wanted to go back to school. And our son was ambivalent. He loved the traveling and that he could learn to speak German by playing with some German kids, instead of struggling with books at school. But he also missed his friends. What should we do? How could we force the children to live a life they didn't want? Even if we knew they would thank us later. As a mother I want my children to be seen, loved, and respected for who they are. I want them to also have a voice.

Then the final battle from the school system came. After three weeks at school, our son had, once again, started to act out. This time he felt falsely accused by a teacher and threw a ball at her. Of course we didn't condone his behavior, but it was easily explained. In the new semester they had merged two classes together so now they were almost twenty students. Our son was heartbroken. He felt powerless, that no one would to listen to him. That was the final straw. We took him out of school immediately.

That same night, I was cried for my son, for his sadness and desperation. What about our responsibilities as adults to protect our children? Shouldn't we support and help them to be the best they can be? Why are millions of children diagnosed daily with different diseases? There is nothing wrong with the children! It is a flaw with society and a school system that wants to fit them into a box.

This was when Bhagavan appeared to me in a vision. He said:

Sanna, time has come. You are ready for your mission. You have been tested and trained your whole life. You passed your tests. Now you are going to bark on the journey toward your mission. You are going to create a new Global One World School System. Just follow my guidance. Act when you are guided to. You don't have to understand how and where you are going. Just trust. We will bring you there.

I have never felt so supported by the universe in my life. I have never trusted so much. My mission is so big that I cannot even try to grasp how it can be manifested. So I *have* to trust. And let myself be guided. I had to let go and let God.

Looking back now, it all makes sense. Why I ended up with two master's degrees, one in Developmental Psychology and one in Education. Why I always wanted to work for children, why I wanted children. My daughter said the other night, *"Mom, when I grow up, I want to work with you and your school system. I want to support you and help children."*

My family believes in me. That makes it easier to take on this mission. But when our world is filled with fear, disasters, wars, and crime, how could I not? How can I leave this world knowing I didn't do everything I could to create a better world for my children and the generations to come?

Learning doesn't have to be one-sided, divided, hard, and boring. Learning is supposed to be fun, inclusive, and expansive. We must break free from the old systems and paradigm that no longer work. We have to start from scratch and create a foundation where children thrive and can save the planet where we have failed. It's up to them to create peace on earth. How could you ever go to war with someone you go to school with? Children are not born racists, evil, or bad. That is taught.

There is a new generation of children on the planet. Children, who see the world differently than we did back in the days. Children, that are seen as different and even not "normal." Children, who have more developed brains than many adults, and who have more activated DNA. Some are called "smarter," some are called "different." Some are called indigo, star or crystal children. We incorrectly label these children as wrong. We even give them an "alphabet" diagnosis—ADHD, Autism, Asperger's, Bipolar, Explosive, Hyperactive, Sensitive…

What if it is the *system* that does not fit a new generation of children? What if *we* are trying to put them into a box they do not fit in? The school system is not equipped to teach the children who are outside of the "norm." Subsequently, they are under-stimulated or over-stimulated, medicated, ostracized, and everything in between. Preschool teachers, kindergarten teachers, and parents are told to work on integrating the children into a school system. How can *three year old kids* prepare for school—to sit quietly, listen deeply, and nod at all the right times? How can they learn to read, write, and count before they can walk? This is what I want to change.

What if we are "wrong" as adults? What if we are the ones to change the system to fit the new generation, instead of trying to make them fit into our old one—one that isn't working? What if we started to see the new generation—our children, who are taking over this world—as equals, or even as our *teachers*? Instead of seeing them as wrong, we should see the perfection in them, their potential. What if we let them learn *when* they wanted, *what* they wanted, *how* they wanted, and trust and support them in *their exploration* of the world? I am not suggesting leaving children totally in charge of their education, but that we create a *framework* where *they* can have a say in *how* they learn. This is the hope of a new Global One World School System, one where we have the chance to create a new paradigm in education that can change the world for generations to come. This is my mission. I know that now.

Love cannot be fit into any box of reason or understanding. It is the light of grace through which every soul is liberated from its self-imposed box of limiting reasons and self-defeating understandings. Love cannot accommodate the preferences of prisoners. It is simply too busy setting hearts free, so that all are free to love.

~ Matt Kahn

About the Author

Susana Mei is a passionate Transformational-Author, Speaker, Retreat Designer, and Facilitator. She creates Global Tailored retreats, workshops and events. Susana teaches Heart Empowerment, Flow Schooling, Holistic Health, and Compassionate Leadership, and specializes in inspiring and transforming a new generation of conscious heart-centered light workers who want to make a difference in the world to overcome their limitations and fears and live their lives to the fullest potential being joyful, empowered and free.

She is the author of *Flow Food, Goodness, Grace and Great Thoughts on Fire,* and the forthcoming book *From Money with Love. She is also the* co-author of *No Mistakes.*

Susana Mei is happily married to Oliver and is the joyful proud mother of three children. Together, they travel the world—activating Heart Light Energy, Flow Schooling their children, and embodying a life beyond their wildest dreams.

To find out more, go to: TheosHeart.com

The Power of Love

Sólveig Þórarinsdóttir

My journey of transforming from being a badass banker into something way, way different started off with a visit to my grandparents. I was in the north of Iceland, a few years ago, in the countryside.

My grandfather was, at the time close to 100 years old, 98 to be exact. My grandmother is 10 years younger, of course. □ He is almost blind, but he smiles with his eyes. He is tall, has glowing white hair and when he walks, he moves slowly, but his back is straight. He is at least as graceful as Grace Kelly ever was.

My grandmother could be a 'poster-woman' for the concept of the warm mother. When she hugs you, you just sink into her chubby body and big boobs. You feel safe and at home.

I'd love to be like that when I become a grandmother, one day.

Well, I was there in their kitchen, in their old house where they gave birth to, and brought up, 10 children. We were having a conversation. I was at the end of my pregnancy with my youngest child, had one infant in my arms and one toddler running around my legs.

My grandmother looked me in the eyes and said to me *"Sól, you are becoming just like me when I was your age!"* I looked at her, thinking. 'She's gone crazy now.'

"Amma, how can you say that? You gave birth to 10 babies in 14 years and this is only my third one?!" *And my last one!* But I kept that thought to myself.

"Well you are living in new times. You have countless roles in life that I did not have. Women of your time are all super humans!" she said.

My grandmother looked at my grandfather, with love in her eyes. They giggled, happy, almost 10 decades old. Still in love with each other.

I felt this amazing feeling, like electric fire going through my entire body. From top, down. I felt completely grounded. Time stood still, as I watched them. I saw that the alternative to everything stressful is **LOVE**.

And I dearly wanted the same! I wanted, at their age, to be at that stage in life, to be able to look back and be really proud of my legacy. And still be passionate, giving and energetic.

I knew at this moment, and I felt it in every cell, that if I continued my lifestyle something would break and probably the first thing to leave would be my health. I had this true moment of clarity, which I knew I had to follow with action.

The Shift

I was running from one task to another, putting out fires everywhere, doing a double the regular job at a resolution committee in one of the national banks in Iceland. This was during the financial crisis. I was finishing my master's degree in finance at the same time, having three children in four plus years, with my partner flying abroad in rescue missions for the Icelandic Coastguard, half the year. I did not know how, or even want to, ask for help. That's not what we Alpha women do!

At this moment in time, in my grandparent's kitchen, everything became clear to me. I didn't even know that things weren't clear before!! *Me! **WHAT!** Not clear?*

I, who had my life and everything perfectly figured out. Carefully calculated in an excel spreadsheet, everything in sync on my various I-devices!

Long story short: I returned back home a new person. Or better yet, the same person, but one who had found her true purpose.

The very next day I resigned from my job. Most people thought I'd gone mad. Who would give up this amazing high-paid career? At these critical times! I told my friends in the banking sector, without any hesitation, that I would not be taking any job calls for the next two years, at the very least.

I decided to take responsibility for this young family I had just started. I decided that I would trust in my insight and my heart, that I would be shown the next steps, in my new journey.

This was a totally new way of thinking for me, after all, I had previously tried to control and bend everything to my will.

I'm often asked if doing this didn't take a lot of courage. The answer is no. It just felt so **right**. I could feel my heart shouting, YES! The funny thing is that this came suddenly, without notice. It surprised me at the time.

Now I know that the Universe reveals its secrets to those who dare to follow their heart.

If I would not have taken action at that time this would just have been another mundane conversation or activity in everyday life. Later, I realized that a moment of clarity followed by lack of action is nothing but a thought gone with the wind.

Please do not let those moments pass you by or slip through your fingers. They can be so utterly transformative and life changing.

I did not let that moment go by unnoticed. For that I will be forever grateful!

A few days later, after this life-changing journey to my homestead, I delivered my youngest child.

The Challenge

But then what?! I just stood in my pajamas, barefoot in the laundry room in the middle of the day folding countless socks of children with no plan! Except for listening to my heart from now on… *Were they all right? Had I gone mad or somewhat crazy? What about my world domination plan in the financial sector? What about my high-end lifestyle?* No income, no nothing! Burning up all my life savings.

Ah but no, that feeling of conviction that I was finally doing what ever it took to be aligned with my true self was my saving grace. Now I was putting an end to the all the deep, deep suffering. And few week's later, **BOOM:** I started practicing yoga.

I found yoga or yoga found me.

On the mat I could feel how far I'd been away from my authentic self. Yoga and meditation became the lifeline in my transformational journey. It was a point of no return for me so I travelled to various continents to seek deeper knowledge and became a teacher, as I couldn't wait to share everything I was feeling with others. I wrote a best selling yoga book, opened the Solir Yoga and Health center in Reykjavik, Iceland, a platform for people to **heal**.

Still, the struggle was real. It's not easy to make a 180 degree U-turn. I did suffer, a lot. Yes, I do know it's not easy for everyone to see or understand all that suffering, when my life on paper looked so amazingly fitted to society's rules and standards.

My life did have its dark side. One that had it's basic root in the fact that my existence was too one dimensional. I took no joy out of any of it. I was so unbalanced because I was neither aware of, nor fulfilling my real needs in life.

For example my temper was literally on fire. I had to put so much energy into not blowing like the traditional Icelandic volcanos all the time.

One memorable morning at home, in a typical family situation, stands out for me. Everyone needs to be up in the morning to dress, brush teeth, comb hair, eat breakfast, find school books and gym bags, let the cat out, do all the usual family stuff. Finally, when everything is ready, the youngest knocks over a liter of milk, all over the table, the other kids and me. As I, the mother, sit there, the cat likes what's going on, so she jumps on the table, and starts to dance in the puddle of milk. *The best cat morning ever!*

Heavy silence descends. The kids look up, fear in their eyes. Will mother explode? She looks back, drenched in milk. Instead of allowing disappointment, frustration and thoughts of all the bad consequences take over, something else happens. I see the fear. The expectation that now I will be shouting at them. Because of what? Because an infant spilled milk?!

No. Not this time. I watch myself, from a distance. I become a silent witness. I smile at the kids, clean up the mess, find new clothes. World War 3 was averted!

This is how the most mundane event can lead to illumination. If this is possible once, if I can stay a silent witness, in difficult situations, once and then twice, then it is here to stay. I stop being thoughtless and poisoning my relationships.

It was yoga that taught me mindfulness. Yoga introduced to me the silent witness concept.

The Solution, the connection with my root

That led back to my grandparents. Again. I had lost the connection with my roots.

I spent a lot of time with my grandparents when I was a child. The memories I have are so beautiful.

When I think back I see this little girl, running in the green grass, so fast and so fearless. I can smell the memory of the summers when my family was out in the fields, working with the animals, milking, harvesting, doing all these chores you do on a farm.

I can still see myself, long blond hair, sun kissed cheeks, bare feet, dirty toes, playing music on my pocket radio for the cows, trying to get them to dance and be happy with me. Big, fat, juicy cows, rocking to a Prince Song,

'You don't have to be rich, to be my girl, you don't have to be beautiful...' This is who I truly am, that little happy, bright soul.

My grandparents **NEVER** raised their voice to any children. Everything they did, said and taught, was from pure love. Even if they had 10 children and have since over 80 plus descendants! It sounds impossible not to have any conflict in that big a family, for such a long time. But that's true.

What I learned from them, is that if your acts come from the pure intention of love, conflicts will resolve themselves or just never appear. We will suffer less, fight less. If I may quote our beloved Martin Luther King, Jr., *"Darkness cannot drive out darkness, only light can do that. Hate cannot drive out hate, only love can do that."*

Is it possible for us to transform our lives, by simply changing our perspectives? Yes, we can, all of us, if we find our true purpose! For me, the root is love, that's the key to the solution.

The negative me

Having read the above you may think me a lucky person, a ray of sunshine; great grandparents, wise mother and daughter, happy marriage, successful career. All true. But there is also the other side.

I am also a sensitive and emotional person. I tend to be obsessive. Yeah, working double shifts in the banking sector, finishing a degree, given birth to three kids, pilot husband away at work. Juggling all of these balls and more all at the same time. Easy, peazy! Impossible, if not for the obsessive, over-achieving, 'you can do it' girl, just push some more, wring x% more energy out of your soul, ask the almighty to add extra hours to the day.

Yeah. I've hurt myself so many times. I have suffered. I have thought: *This is not the way to live.* I have even felt suicidal, I'm sorry to say.

The simple fact is that we can never hide from ourselves. We may abuse alcohol and food, overeat, over train or any kind of absence in any of our 'drug' of choice.

What to do? - How did I heal myself?

For me the start is love. Love is the power that unifies us, the power that says, 'lets work together, resolve our conflicts, and respect each other.'

When I woke up to the Power of Love I realized that I need and want to serve. At the same time I realize that when I open my heart and I start giving, everything that's meant to come, will come to me.

How do we turn up the 'love'!

Before I start on that I want to say that **I'm not naive**. I'm a former badass banker. Never forget that. I worked for over ten years in that sector. I've seen how people in power act. I know we have a lot of work in front of us.

However, I believe that if we want to save this world, to hand it over intact to our children and grandchildren, we have to start somewhere. We can't just give up, roll over and hand the world to people whom say: 'If you screw me, I'll screw you ten times over.'

So, what do I need to do? I must fall in love with myself. I must be the love of my life. Again, this may sound 'cheesy', but this is the truth. How can I give love if I have no love to give? How can I love you, if I hate or disrespect me? I can't. I'll start disrespecting you, because there must be something wrong with you to love me.

To increase love we need to work. We humans are like a garden. To stay healthy—to live in the highest dimension of our possibilities, we need to cultivate our body, our mind, our heart, and our soul. Every day of our lives. If you thing your are done, good luck with that!

To really help others we have to love ourselves, learn to be at ease in our own skin. My own experience, from reading, observing life and working in the business community, is that conflicts come from dis-contentment, being ill at ease in your skin, frustrations and anger leads to eruptions, to **WAR**.

No conditions

I also think that the core of human drama is conditional love. I love you **IF** ... you cook my favorite dinner, do this ... for me, or ... enter you own experiences.

The problem is that we love ourselves, with lots of conditions attached! *I'm happy because I've earned x dollars this month, because he praised me, because she did not scold me, because I've exercised every day of the week.* And the next week I disrespect myself, because I ate too much chocolate, didn't deliver in some way, only went twice to the gym, he did not say that he loves me! Oh...

We need to find the way to unconditional love. We need to unlearn the belief system which is keeping us stuck in suffering.

It is time to embrace the facts, and it's the truth: I am completely perfect just the way I am. This is what we, each of us, need to understand.

You don't need anybody but you. You are love. Love is within you. You need no guru, no teacher. It's all within. However, we need friends. People who support us. People we support. After all. Life is one. We are all the same. It is already there.

That's what I'm working towards. And it is a never ending journey.

To maintain resilience and balance I now use Natures Genetics, a wonderful program called VIE!

We are part of nature. VIE stands for Vitality, Intellect and Emotions. The VIE program analyses my personality and tells me how I am innately. This helps me understand who I am, the whole of my personality. It encourages me to accept myself and that in turn leads to freedom. Last but not least, it helps me maintain a healthy balance, because it reminds me of all the aspects to my personality.

Like I have already said, being the best version of myself, is very important, for me, for my family and for my work. To heal the world, we have to start with ourselves. An old, and maybe overused phrase, but true nonetheless!

When I am a pure and clear resource of love, I channel the beauty of all life.

About the Author

Sólveig Þórarinsdóttir is the founder and owner of Solir, Yoga and health Center, Reykjavik. She is the author of the best-seller, Yoga for All and co-authoring the books *Time to Rise and Resilience Through Yoga and Meditation*. She is a dedicated wellness and health fanatic, leading Icelanders by her example. She is also married to Holmar and a mother of three wonderful children.

Learn more at www.Solir.is and www.NatureGenetics.me

What Extended Unemployment Taught Me About the Law of Attraction

Julia Aarhus

Life simply does not always progress the way you planned or dreamt of, does it?

I certainly did not plan on my mother dying suddenly at the age of 57 after only four weeks of illness and without knowing what her diagnosis was. And I definitely didn't plan to be unemployed for a LONG time, TWICE (1½ and 2 years) in the wake of dealing with my mother's departure from this world.

No, I did not plan or wish for any of that. Not in my right mind would I have planned for any of those challenges and struggles. And I struggled—a lot!

Grieving the loss of loved ones is, of course, a perfectly natural process and an expression of love. But there is normal grieving, and then there is struggle. And a year later, I was still struggling to come to terms with my mother's sudden death, which made being a mother to an infant and a toddler very hard.

I was 20 weeks pregnant, and my firstborn was barely 14 months old when my mother died. I was a high-tempered, short-fused basket case, feeling like life had caught me off guard. My trust in life, which was clearly not on my side anymore, was broken. I felt like a victim of life's cruelty. My stress level was sky high, and every day I felt that I was harming my kids and jeopardizing their healthy development, which caused more stress, which then again jeopardized my own health even further. You get the picture...

This state continued when my maternity leave ended and both my girls were in daycare. Don't get me wrong; time did heal some of the pain connected to losing my mother and it did do me good to

[handwritten: Whate is the Joy in my forces]
[handwritten: Where is the Light]

Joy Light Works

[handwritten: How Does It Work]

~~Finding joy in adversity;~~ the
journey to healing chronic illness
using a whole-being approach

Consulting and Advocacy for patients,
families, and providers within the
fields of Functional Medicine and
Biological Dentistry. *[handwritten: & including]*

[handwritten: Non-Toxic]

[handwritten: define]

What clients have said about Karan;

"...is compassionate and helped me to cope with an unbearable situation...she helped me believe in the power of my own choices"

"...referred me to a Biological Dentist after 2yrs of trying to save a dead root canal tooth. My health was suffering and within two weeks, the tooth was extracted. My fatigue improved within 3wks."

"...was able to help my husband understand that his sleep apnea was impacting my health due to stress and insomnia. He agreed to a sleep study test and was found to have severe apnea. He was treated with an oral dental appliance and we are both healthier and more rested today"

"...was there for me when I did not want to live anymore. We were able to figure out how my life long thoughts and beliefs were impacting my ability to recover because she understood without judging me"

Contact Me

Karan Joy Almond
Columbia, Maryland

karan@joylightworks.com

443-583-9975

have some weight and responsibilities lifted off my shoulders between 9 a.m. and 3 p.m. Monday to Friday, but those hours were spent looking for a job and receiving one rejection letter after another. This went on for 1½ years and I felt more and more unworthy of actually landing that dream job—or any job for that matter. Worthless, useless, shameful, unfulfilled, sad, angry, restless, you name it! What was ever to become of me? And why me? What was I doing wrong?

What WAS I doing wrong…? At this point, I had watched both *The Secret and What the bleep do we know more than once.* Both films talk about the Law of Attraction and how everything is energy and that like attracts like. This means we can raise the frequency of our energy or vibe and thereby attract the same higher frequency. This is scientifically proven.

The Secret explains how to imagine, visualize, dream and feel how great it will be to get that dream job or car or house, etc., and I was doing all of that alongside applying for several jobs a week, but nothing happened for 1½ years.

All I was longing for was a job that would be somewhat fulfilling and meaningful. I was sure that a job would be my salvation from this horrific limbo, but this was in 2008 – 2009, and due to the Financial Crisis, jobs weren't hanging from the trees.

I was ecstatically happy and jumping for joy when I was finally offered a job in June 2009. I think I might have been crying tears of joy as well. I was certainly calling and texting EVERYBODY to share my wonderful news.

The job was great in the beginning and I thought and felt that I would evolve in this place for years. This was it! My luck had finally turned.

Six months in, the work environment became more and more stressful. To cut a long story short, I resigned due to health reasons, which turned out to be a relief. A little over a year earlier, I thought unemployment was the worst possible scenario. Now I knew that being in a stressful job was worse. Man, I was bad at that Law of Attraction thing!

Or, it was just not meant to be. The Universe and my soul had other plans for me. That's what I tried to tell myself.

For years I believed that I had a soul but I had not yet figured out nor decided on what that meant. I had not yet found an explanation that rang true to me. That came later, in 2012, during my second period of extended unemployment. This was after another job, one that I also thought was IT. But when business declined, I was let go. In truth, I had already felt that this job as a receptionist would soon bore me and that a new desire was stirring in me.

In August 2012, I became a certified life coach and the training was life-changing for me. I got to know myself on a whole new level, and the raised awareness sure came in handy in dealing with that second round of extended unemployment. This time around, I was not suffering to the same extent as the first time. This time around, I was aware of how unemployment didn't do a very good job in meeting my basic human needs. I knew it was up to me to actively have them fulfilled elsewhere. I realized how I had been attached to a job giving me Certainty, both financially and personally. I had been attached to a job making me feel *Significant* and *Connected*, and a job being the source of experiencing *Growth*. And I realized how this attachment had left me feeling like a victim.

Another thing—and the most important thing—that coach training taught me was the power of beliefs and how to detect and question my beliefs.

Beliefs are the truths we have convinced ourselves of—consciously or unconsciously. They are simply thoughts, and those thoughts beliefs/truths are what affect our individual experience of an event. Ultimately, they decide our reality.

The truth you hold about, say, unemployment sets off specific thoughts about it, which triggers specific emotions about it, which determines your experience of it and thereby your reality.

In short: Truth → Thought → Emotion → Experience → Reality

I have sat through enough coaching sessions, on both sides of the table, to verify that this is how it works and that we have a strong tendency to believe our imagined truths to be universal laws. I am amazed how much imagined crap we convince ourselves of, and I love how some inquiry can make an imagined truth fall apart and appear to be exactly that.

The truth I held about unemployment was that it was not supposed to be. It was my enemy and something I had to avoid or fight and shorten the time frame of at any cost and. This truth naturally made me feel horrible, and I learned that it was highly influenced and fueled by the opinions shouted out by politicians and the media. It was clearly also the opinion of the average population. The words and facial expressions said it all when people learned about my unemployment: That's not good, that's too bad, what a shame! And ashamed was what this attitude, this belief, made me feel. Ashamed and wrong. I thank God, literally, that I stumbled upon the work of Brené Brown sometime during 2012. I read two of her books on dealing with shame and daring to be vulnerable—and they did wonders for me.

The first step away from this belief and toward making peace with unemployment was, for me, becoming aware of it. The next step was an overhaul and an expansion of my belief system about life and being human in general. I finally found that explanation—of what it means to have a soul—that rang true to me, and through that my understanding of the Law of Attraction, I was given a new depth and angle. I found a peace I had never known before.

I made complete peace with being unemployed only a few months before I reached the limit of collecting money from the unemployment fund. I came to believe that unemployment was what my soul had chosen for me at this point in my life and that it was serving a higher good. I had faith that, in time, I would be able to connect the dots and see the meaning to it. I believed that what appeared to be things falling apart were really things *falling together*. I believed all was well.

Four books, a two-day workshop, and writing a book made the difference. The books were: *Conversations with God* 1, 2 and 3 and *The Only Thing That Matters*, all written by Neale Donald Walsch. The workshop was also with Neale and the book I wrote was a direct result of meeting Neale and that workshop. Though it is not published...yet, writing it was the greatest thing ever.

Let me take you back to the first morning of that workshop on October 8th, 2013. In fact, I almost didn't attend because I really couldn't afford it.

Neale had been talking about creating your own reality and had said something like: Most of what we create is created at a subconscious level. (He later got into how we create our own inner reality by choosing our beliefs and truths, but this part was about the creation of exterior events.) I raised my hand and asked, "at a subconscious level?" Then what was left for me to consciously do to attract what I desired? At this point, I was 15 months into my second period of unemployment. Once again, I had been working the Law of Attraction the best I could and I had, of course, put a lot of action into landing that dream job. And once again, nothing seemed to happen. So, I wanted to know, from the man who speaks directly to God, how big a percentage of creation can I affect with my conscious mind and my actions?

I asked, "You said that most of what we create, we create at a subconscious level, and I would like to know—because I've been unemployed for 15 months and I have been working my butt off to consciously attract a job that I will love—what CAN I do? (My intention was to ask how big a percentage—give or take—of creation I could affect with my conscious mind. But before I knew it, Neale started asking me questions in return.)

He asked if he could do "soul-logic" with me, and I agreed.

Neale asked: Do you believe in God/something higher?

I answered: Yes.

Neale asked: Do you believe you have a soul?

I answered: Yes.

Neale asked: What do you believe the relationship between God and your soul is?

I answered: It's the same (meaning my soul is an individuation of God).

Neale asked: Do you believe anything bad can happen to God?

I answered: No—I think God has that covered.

Neale asked: Given that your soul and God are the same, do you believe anything bad can happen to you?

I answered: No.

Neale asked: What is then the good thing about being unemployed for this extended period of time?

I answered, crying: I get to have more time with my kids (a shift in energy took place across the room at this point).

Neale said, calmly: The soul speaks in tears. That's the agenda of your soul; to spend time with your children.

Then Neale said, focused and very direct at me, "So you'll write a book. A book titled: *Finding Work is Pointless*. With the subtitle: How to deal with extended unemployment. You'll send it to me by the 1st of February at the latest. If later, I will not read it. If I receive it by the 1st of February, I'll read it, and if I like it, I'll write the foreword to it, and I will send it to my Danish publisher with my recommendation. Your soul has been longing to write a book for a while—and you know that."

I answered, nodding and sobbing, "Yes!"

Then Neale went on to explain how all creation is co-creation and how any event is created by all the souls who are and ever will be affected by the event.

A-HA!!! I got it. The souls of my two beautiful, delicate but strong daughters had, without a doubt, been co-creators of their mother not getting any of those many, many jobs she applied for. That extra time and presence I had with my daughters through my extended periods of unemployment could not be measured in relation to our tight financial situation or the number of rejection letters I received. Everything else faded and meant so little compared to all those extra hours spent with my children. I did not always see that, but now I did. One shift in perspective and my suffering and desperation ended. Wow!

And it is not just that—not to belittle the importance of what I just wrote about my children— there were so many times during my unemployment when I was able to be there on the spot for a friend in need because I managed my own time. Those friends were also co-creators of my unemployment. You, reading this, my contribution to Time to Rise, were also co-creating it at a subconscious-soul-level. And any future reader of the book I wrote, that Neale did write a beautiful foreword for, were also co-creators of it. The list goes on and on, beyond what my human imagination can come up with.

This perspective, this insight, this belief made me RISE. It made me feel worthier than ever before because I realized my worth in this world had nothing to do with the title I held, or the job I had, or the money I earned, etc. From that moment on, my favorite quote became this:

"Your life has nothing to do with you. It has to do with everyone whose life you touch."
~ Neale Donald Walsch

Not that I am not important. On the contrary. If I am to touch potentially many lives in a significant way, I do need to take care of myself and be true to myself. I have to take care of my human needs, select my beliefs and my values consciously, and dare to be vulnerable and put myself out there. I need to be connected to the subtle voice of my soul speaking to me in feelings, signs and intuition. When I balance those two aspects of being me, the human and the spiritual part, and when I keep in mind that we are all connected and co-creators of each other's lives, then I am most capable of touching lives.

Extended unemployment gave me the necessary space, time and opportunity to RISE to that realization. And alongside that, I got to spend a lot more time with my children when they were little. What a dream come true, really. Thank you for that!

PS: That Law of Attraction is not fake. It's just a little more complex than what I first learned about it. Because there are other laws of this universe too and sometimes what we are trying to manifest is overruled by the agendas of our souls. This doesn't mean that we should stop trying to manifest our dreams and desires. On the contrary. But the trick is to know the agenda of your soul and have that become what you also work on manifesting from a conscious level. In my perspective, anyway.

121

About the Author

Julia Aarhus lives in Denmark with her husband and their two daughters. She is a trained teacher and life coach and she is currently training to be a family counselor. She is passionate about coaching and educating parents and adults working with children in regards to the new paradigm of pedagogy and child-rearing. A paradigm revolving around authenticity, personal leadership and equality nurturing the integrity of both the child and the adult.

To connect with Julia send an email to juliaaarhus@live.dk or visit https://www.facebook.com/Julia-Aarhus-1963790030555231/

Awakened by My Gifted Kids

Lorena Plæhn

The phone rang and I answered, "It's Lorena."

"Hi, honey, it's Shannie. Where are you?"

"I wrapped up the kids and went for some errands."

"Good idea—the energies are really dancing around in your house. They know we were invited to the party today."

I already knew that without really being aware of it. I just got the thought in my head that it would be good if the kids and I were out of the house until our appointment at 11 a.m.

Shannie continued, "I will be there just before eleven, and Athene might come before me. You have to do one thing for me before I get there. You have to tell Charlie that he is right—there are ghosts in your house."

I hesitated a bit, but she continued: "If you don't do it, I will hunt you down, lady!"

Who wants to be hunted down by a witch? Certainly not me! So, of course, I said yes, wondering how on earth I would tell this to my 11-year-old son without scaring him. Before the thought had come to an end, Shannie said, "And don't you worry about scaring him. He knows, and he understands. Remember, he is much wiser than you on so many levels that you will never understand."

You would think I would have gotten used to Shannie reading my thoughts, knowing her for at least a couple of years and having used her as our personal spiritual advisor and shaman, but no! It always surprised me that she was so tuned in to situations.

So, I went home with the kids (my step-daughter aged 17 and son aged 11) with time to spare before the meeting with Shannie and Athene. I took my son and sat him on the kitchen table. I had something to tell him.

"Charlie, I am truly sorry for not having said this before, but you are right—we do have ghosts in our home."

What happened next will always remain in my brain as a crystal-clear image. It will be permanently etched in my mind to remind me to never, ever underestimate any child's observations in life. Especially my own child's observations. NEVER!

Try to imagine a wave of energy flushing in from the top of your child's head, rolling down through his head and face to his shoulders, chest, stomach, hips, legs and feet. Imagine seeing all the tense energy being flushed out through his feet and replaced with relief—pure, clear relief!

I had never seen anything like that before. Standing there, realizing that all my son ever wanted was for me to acknowledge him, his feelings, and his skills—oh my God! I felt like the worst mum ever. And right then and there, my awakening started for real.

Years earlier

When Charlie was one and a half years old, we decided to sell our house and move to a farm further out on the island. This area is 12 km from Copenhagen, the capital of Denmark. And though it is just ten minutes from the airport, it is certainly in the countryside. There is forest, sea, and a big natural area called Faelleden, where cars and other motorized vehicles are not allowed.

Our farm was surrounded by fields, and there are beautiful expanses of nature in all directions from the house. Though I never dreamed of living there, I had this strange feeling the first time I walked into the house that this was it. This was my final destination and the place I would stay until I got old.

Despite this feeling, it quickly became clear to us that this house had a lot of mixed energies and ghosts trying to be expressed in one way or another. We knew that the former owner had committed suicide in the house, and we could feel his pain in the energy of the house. My husband was especially attuned to him and could feel his presence.

At first, we didn't take any of it seriously. When the kids tried to talk to us about the strange things they felt in the house, we told them that they had nothing to be afraid of. Thus, we never really knew what they saw or felt. We always simply dismissed their reports, thinking that it would be best if we convinced them that it was only ghost stories and nothing to be afraid of.

But over the years, it continued to intensify. It culminated with Charlie not wanting to be in his room—or left alone in any room—after dark. He didn't even want to go to the toilet on his own, and he became more and more terrified of being at home alone at any time of the day. Even guests visiting our house expressed that they felt strange things going on.

Finally, we decided to seriously investigate the problem. We hired a clairvoyant to come to the house and explore the issue. She gave us a lot of information and informed us that she had cleared it for us, but she hadn't. So, we kept searching for a solution.

One day, I had arranged a fun clairvoyance evening with some friends at our home. One of them had been in contact with a shamanic woman named Shannie and had booked her to come and "entertain" us for the evening.

Shannie arrived as agreed, but when I opened the door for her, I noticed that she had parked her car in the middle of our yard—not to the side, not at the end, but right in the middle. I asked her to move her car so my husband could easily access the garage if he came home before she left. She looked at me with a terrified expression and said:

"Are you out of your mind? I cannot park my car anywhere else on this farm without being afraid of what will happen to it! This farm is insanely haunted!"

Welcome to my home!

Over the curse of that night, I learned a lot about energies, and about my home and the ground it was built on. I was not necessarily happy about the information I learned that evening. The good thing, though, was that she was also a "housecleaner." She could help us clean the house of unwanted energies and give it protection from future energies that might come to our home. I trusted her.

This brings us to our appointment many years later. The one where she told me to acknowledge my son! On this particular day, she came and did the housecleaning and put up protection. She arrived with a colleague to complete the work. The things they did and told us that day really turned our world upside down, completely convincing us that there truly was more going on than meets the eye. I realized that I couldn't continue to ignore my son's skills or the things that had been going on in our house.

When Shannie and Athene were done, Shannie asked me to make an appointment with Charlie. She told me that she needed to find out what exactly his gifts and talents were to give him and us some clarity on how we could support him in the future.

The appointment with Charlie was mind-blowing—for her, him and me. His skills were tremendous. It turned out that ghosts and energies were seeking him out, trying to be rescued and helped to move on from where they were stuck. I had no clue whatsoever how to support him in working with these skills. Or what to do if he didn't want to be contacted or provide help. Or how to open or close these energies. Or if you could even do that. I had no clue.

That was when I decided that I had to do something different with my life so I could support my son on this journey. From being the head of administration in a small company, I had already decided to become a psychotherapist to help my step-daughter with some different issues. I had gotten a job as a chief executive secretary and signed up for a four-year course of education. But now, two years later, I realized that it wasn't enough. If I was to truly understand, I had to also educate myself in spirituality, so I signed up for a private education as a spiritual mentor in addition to my continued education as a psychotherapist. I finally completed both at the same time in 2013.

Though the decision about helping my son was a point of no return for me, becoming a Spiritual Mentor opened all the doors to my awakening and made me realize that this was really all about my own need to find my own truth and rise to shine.

The beautiful journey into the universal laws, contact with angels, energy and soul work, light and dark energy, shamanism, clairvoyance, healing, crystals, tarot cards, angel cards, astrology, nature, paganism, and much, much more felt so right and beautiful to my soul.

In 2012, early in this spiritual adventure, I gathered my family for a small family meeting. I asked them if they were content with the way we lived our lives—because I sure wasn't. Up until that point, it had been all about coping and just getting by, concentrating on earning money and helping our kids with whatever needs they had. At that point, my spiritual journey had revealed to me that there was another way. A much more pleasant and satisfactory way to live.

So, I asked my husband and kids what they dreamed of. I introduced vision boards for everybody.

And I "commanded" them to watch *The Secret* with me and discuss it afterward. That was the real point of no return for my family and me. From then on, I could not go back to live my life the old way. It was impossible.

I changed my working hours from a full-time job to a part-time job so I could start having clients. I figured that if I could do that for some years, I could build up my clinic at my own pace and someday skip my part-time job.

During these years, Charlie had said that he wanted to spend a year as an exchange student in the USA. We were surprised because he had always been the more quiet and shy type, but we also recognized that, since his journey into himself and his own acknowledgment of his skills and talents, major shifts had happened with him. So, we sent him off to the USA for high school.

It was a tough time for me. I had spent so many years focusing on my kids and their needs, and my son had been the driving force behind my spiritual shift and my new way of living. So, to be completely frank, I felt pretty lost and abandoned when he left. My step-daughter had already moved away from home years earlier, so the house was very quiet in the beginning. But it would turn out to be a huge advantage.

Three months after he left, I got fired from my job. I can't say that I was unhappy about it, but I was shocked because my plan had been to stick to it for at least one or two more years. Apparently, that was not how my life was supposed to turn out.

Both my husband and I felt it was a major setback to our own plans; so in the beginning, we were worried. However, as you might already know, the Universe always has our backs—and this was no exception. I received four months of salary without having to show up at the office, and since Charlie was being taken care of in the USA, I had time to put all my energy into my clinic and all kinds of studies. So, I did. And, within these four months, I managed to build up my clinic from a part-time job to a full-time job. It was meant to be!

My awakening has been like traveling through time, and it has been one of the most beautiful, eye-opening, frustrating, and hardest things I have ever done, next to becoming a mum without knowing myself and my dreams for real. It started by becoming a psychotherapist and traveling back to my childhood and teenage life to clean up myself and my convictions about life.

Right after going into spiritual study and working with my soul, I started talking to my "real" parent—God! I found out that I am so much more than what meets the eye. That has really been a mind-blowing and tough journey.

Going through all these processes is kind of like being dressed wrong all the time. You think you've found the perfect dress and the perfect shoes for the ball, and then, while walking out the door, you realize that your dress is already outdated and you have to go shopping for a new one. Now, some would think that buying dresses is great fun, but if you never really get the chance to wear them before you have to find a new one, AND you run around naked in the meantime, that is not fun at all!

While writing this, I feel cleaned up and put together. I have found my dress—and it is very, very beautiful. I am still on a journey of exploration because awakening is not about being done. Awakening or rising is, for me, all about coming forth as the real me. It means daring to shine my true light and become the beacon others can use to find their harbor or the right stores with the right dresses. That is what my business and life are all about today. I help people tap into their true identity and shine their true light in the world.

The world needs us, and the world needs each loving contribution to life it can get. Even though the road is full of bumps and twists and turns, I can assure you that doing it is worthwhile.

It really is time to rise for all of us.

About the Author

Lorena Plæhn is a spiritual warrior, mother and wife. Her mission in this life is to lift and empower others. Lorena is a psychotherapist, spiritual mentor and a transformational leader who helps people find their truth and transform their lives accordingly. She provides psychotherapy, spiritual mentoring, soul readings and astrological character readings to empower people with their true identity and character. In her business, she offers 1:1 sessions, and she facilitates workshops on transformational leadership and empowerment topics.

Lorena has been happily married for 21 years and has been with her husband for 25 years. She has a step-daughter aged 25 years and a son aged 19 years.

Read all about Lorena and her business here: lorenasuniverse.com

Bridging the Gap Between the Generations

Dr. "Juicy" Jill Stocker

When I was a little girl I was well-behaved and looked like a little girl "should." One day I received on my report card of straight "A's" a comment: "Talks too much in class." I now wonder if that was when I started to shut down? Or was it when I was five years old and my mother walked in on me being molested by a neighbor? Afterward she and I both stood there frozen as my dad punched a hole in the wall. But sadly nothing further was discussed about it.

Fast forward to my first women's sharing circle meditation. We did a group meditation and then each woman shared why they were there, and talked about what particular challenges she was currently facing. There were common themes of "not enoughness" and "not being truly seen." I sat frozen as I listened. Many of them had the same demons I carried in my head, heart, and soul. I had thought I was just too sensitive, too emotional, too *much*, yet still not *enough*. I didn't think I'd be able to share, because I was so shaken inside at what I was witnessing. There was such pure vulnerability that it felt like I was being released from my inner prison. When I first began to speak, my voice was shaky, and I was afraid to "sound silly," or "crazy," as I had been told in an emotionally and verbally abusive relationship. I had tears that I had no explanation for, and I tried to shut them down and cover my face, because I thought that crying was weak. I'd also been told I was an "ugly crier." Talk about kicking someone while they're down!

That first night ended and my life was forever changed. I couldn't explain what was happening in a clear-cut way, like all the precise research I'd learned in my medical training. I just knew I felt a shift inside, that people were noticing something about me was different—in a good way. It was as if I had been cracked open and things that had been so tightly bound up inside me were finally flowing freely. It felt like I was giving birth to a new me. Well, not a NEW me...the TRUE me, that had gotten buried under everything. This is why I do what I do...so I can help others, who have preconceived notions of how things "should" look or "should" be, realize their true selves and unlock and unleash their full potential for an AMAZING and JUICY life!

Ever since that first powerful experience with true vulnerability, I have completely changed the way I approach myself, life, my children, my relationships, and my clients. I realized that during consultations it felt like I was just going through the motions; like I was reading from some "script" of the old, traditional teachings of medical school. It certainly didn't feel like "me." It felt sterile, and disconnected. Once I started sharing bits and pieces of myself and truly getting *real*, I realized the amazing strength and courage in sharing my/our vulnerability. It literally gives others "permission" to unlock their own prison by *also* sharing their vulnerability. When I first graduated medical school I was young, and a woman, and not taken seriously because of those two things. So I thought sharing any type of personal connection or information would make me even less credible as a physician. Watching Dr. Andrea talk about her depression and "challenges" during her TEDx talk, gave me permission to do so myself...and acknowledging that gift, I continue to pay it forward.

Through this process, and the ensuing sense of awareness I've discovered, I believe I was given so many of my "challenges" in life to be able to share my experience with others and use my platform as a physician to demonstrate the strength and courage in showing vulnerability and authenticity. Sometimes I wonder, *What's so special about what I have to say?* We all have our own unique perspective, our story, and experiences. Fully embracing ourselves and our own inner awesomeness is the key to unlocking our prison. No one else is me or you and that's what makes our stories unique. Letting go of the structure of what things are "supposed" to look like or holding onto a specific outcome, are what limits us. It's okay, actually, it's more than okay to talk about EVERYTHING sex, masturbation, postpartum depression, losing your "mojo" or vitality, loneliness, getting older, or being "stuck" in a life you thought you wanted and realizing you're meant to do something different.

The journey to self-awareness is so many things. It's heartbreaking, it's heart opening, it's scary, it's lonely, it's UNCOMFORTABLE. But by truly getting to know yourself—the icky parts, beautiful parts, funny parts, goofy parts—you become an unstoppable force and truly start living ALL the parts of your life.

We can choose to live from one of two places—love or fear. I lived a fear-based life for so long, as a "traditional" doctor. Too often we live our life by "checking off boxes" (the boxes of what we think we're "supposed to do") and leave the important stuff, the stuff we're passionate about, for last. When I found myself doing this I knew I was done living my old story.

Somebody once told me that I wasn't strong, that I was a "squishy sponge." And I realize now that there is incredible strength in vulnerability and honesty—honesty about yourself, your flaws, your challenges. There is NOTHING weak about that. I used to never cry because I thought not being emotional was being strong, so I held it in. This was something I had learned to do early on in life, through various experiences, and realized I had unwittingly taught it to my daughter. Now, when I see a woman cry, and talk about her challenge and how she's approaching it and trying to overcome it, I never once think that's weak. It takes incredible courage to be so completely open and vulnerable in front of people. There's *nothing* weak about that. When I see other women be emotional I am less afraid to show it myself, Their vulnerability has given me "permission" to do it.

There's so much shame in society about showing emotions, like they are bad. I'm glad to have emotions, to *feel*, because I've felt numb before. I looked happy, everything seemed perfect, I did everything I was supposed to do, but I wasn't LIVING. I wasn't FEELING. And you know what? I would rather have uncomfortable feelings: sadness, anger, fear, love, and feel ALIVE. I would rather feel *something*, than feel *nothing* at all. It's okay for women to have and to show their feelings. And you know what? We don't need to FIX those feelings! Our emotions are not something that needs to be fixed. We have every right to express ourselves, we can cry, we can yell, we can feel. We should acknowledge those feelings and emotions. They are indications of what is going on inside of us and can often direct our actions. Instead of repressing our emotions, explore WHY you're having them. If they are swept under the rug and never acknowledged, or you try to "fix it" without understanding why you're feeling it, it will keep coming up. So, having feelings, and acknowledging that it's okay to have them is the first step to feeling emotionally alive!

My story has really just begun, and is ever-evolving. It started with me following "the plan" of my life as I thought it should be…high school, college, medical school and a doctor at twenty-five, then marriage and kids. I had it all. I should've been happy right? The funny thing is, I didn't even know what made me happy. When someone asked me what I liked to do for fun I didn't have an answer. I started asking myself, "What's my dream?" Not only could I not answer that question, but I was tired all the time. I thought it was "normal" since I was working full time and raising three young children. But then my hair started falling out and I had brain "fog." I had belly fat despite eating well and exercising. And I had zero desire to have sex, and certainly did not FEEL sexy. I had no ZEST for life, and at that point, the word "juicy" was certainly not in my vocabulary. I knew then that I was simply going through the motions, and not truly living.

While I LOVED (and still do!) my kids, I wasn't fully ENJOYING them. Sure we did activities together—school projects, picnics, went on bike rides—but I didn't feel fully PRESENT for them. I often just wanted to lie down and stare at the ceiling. Everything looked great on the OUTSIDE, but on the INSIDE I had no idea who I was, what my dreams were, or what made me feel ALIVE. I knew really only two emotions at the time, feelings of anger, and feeling numb, as though I were dead inside. The usual prescription for anger was antidepressants, which leveled off the anger, but still left that numb dead feeling.

Fast forward to studying hormonal optimization and being a patient in the process. What a change it made in my life! I now have fun, I giggle, I feel "juicy" and enjoy playing with my kids and am fully present with them, whether it is playing with them or teaching them meditation so they can experience awareness at an early age. After seeing how effective hormonal optimization has been, I can now finally answer my kids' question of "What do you do Mommy?" Their father is a surgeon, that's something tangible, they know that he cuts "the bad" things out. I could never answer this question in a way my kids could understand—or anyone else who asked—until I figured it out for myself. But now I have an answer: I help people find themselves. I help them to get their inner glow and their "mojo" back. I help them feel alive, vibrant, and happy, and truly LIVE their lives, not just exist. People who knew me before I knew *myself* would say they could see sadness behind my eyes. I know what they mean because I saw this same "sadness" behind my kids' eyes after their father and I divorced. I am happy to say that after my hormonal optimization treatment, the "sadness behind my eyes" (and my children's) is gone, and we are forging a new path. (My kids have become my greatest teachers. The way they respond to life is exactly how they should. It's what I indirectly teach them, now that I am living life according to a new "plan.")? Necessary now

I hope that by experiencing this shift, through hormonal optimization and self-awareness spiritual work, it enables this generation, the next generation, and the next…to truly live their lives with open lines of communication and less shame about their feelings and emotions. I now consciously CHOOSE to be the *driver*, not the *passenger*, of my life. That crucial difference has taught me an invaluable lesson and it's a message I try to relay to my children and my clients, so they too can reclaim their power, at any age, and write a new part of *their* story.

So many people go through life blindly following whatever plan they created years ago, (or someone created for them). When in reality, the "plan" is ever-changing and ever-evolving, because *we* are ever-changing and ever-evolving. We set goals, and reach them, and then we set new goals. In "following the plan" we have a preconceived notion of how things should look and how things should feel. We think that at a certain age we *should* feel tired and not quite as vital as when we were younger. I'm here to tell you that it doesn't have to be this way. We can feel vital and "juicy" at all ages, even as we mature and go into our golden years. I'm so fortunate to have discovered the field of medicine I'm currently practicing. I have witnessed the physical, emotional, spiritual, mental, and sexual changes firsthand and also through my clients. It's been an AMAZING journey!

Many women, and men, tell their doctors that they're tired, have "brain fog" or don't feel as "sharp" mentally—like "something's off." They've lost their "edge" or "juiciness" and there's been a dip in their vitality, and sex is just not the same. Unfortunately they're told it's just part of getting older or it's "in their heads" and are put on antidepressants, which then make all those symptoms worse. When my mother went through menopause, she was put on antidepressants instead of being hormonally optimized. She had a severe reaction to the medication, ending with me holding her as she cried on her bedroom floor wishing she had the code to the safe so she could get the gun to kill herself.

So many women of my generation, my mother's generation, have been incorrectly medicated and endured "the change" as it was once called without truly discussing what was going on in their bodies, because it was taboo. Well, it's time to open up the conversations and discuss our ever-changing selves. We don't exist in a vacuum, our emotions and our bodies are continually changing physically, hormonally, emotionally, spiritually, sexually—we must *account* for it, *expect* it, and *address* it. I've made it my life's mission to help women (and men!) become the best version of themselves. They can then truly RECLAIM their JUICINESS, EDGE, and VITALITY so that they can discover all the AMAZING things that were not necessarily part of their original "plan" and start truly living their lives out loud.

About the Author

Hi there! I'm Dr Jill. I'm not your traditional doctor. I specialize in Age Management Medicine and Hormonal Optimization. I've made it my life's work to help women (and men!) RECLAIM their sense of self, JUICINESS, EDGE, and VITALITY! As early as your late twenties, hormones that are VITAL to truly LIVING your life, start to decline and need to be corrected to get you back to the best YOU I know you can be. I'm here to help! My goal is to help you achieve the best version of yourself physically, mentally, emotionally, spiritually, and sexually!

I create a safe space to talk about things that are often deemed embarrassing or shameful, but are so crucial to our overall sense of self and being. I want to help you to truly take charge of your vitality and sexuality, to show you how to achieve the beautiful masterpiece of YOU!

Please find me here: http://www.jillstocker.com/

3

HITTING RESET

Life's Not All Rainbows and Orgasms

Dr. Gayle Friend

"You're nothing but an ice queen," the hiss of my now-ex-husband's venomous words stopped me cold. (Pun intended.) Everything was falling apart. I had the marriage, the house, the two kids—I even had the dog—but I was miserable. How did I get here? How did I go from loving sex to being a bitter, resentful ice queen? The answer to those questions was rooted firmly in a childhood trauma that left me feeling abandoned, sad, and alone.

I didn't experience a lot of love growing up. I knew at a cognitive level that I was loved but I didn't feel it in my body and soul. Performance, accomplishments, keeping up appearances, and religion were what mattered in my family. I was starved for love and to feel accepted for who I was. I had no clue about how to fit in, and when I was older I used sex as a vehicle to find love and feel connected. I thought that if I could provide the best sexual experience then I would be loved, desired, and they'd want to be with me exclusively. In my mind I imagined that I'd have the best relationship because I would be all that my partner would ever want and we would fulfill each other's every dream forever and ever. Amen.

How'd that work out for me? I got a big old "F" for FAIL.

So, what did I do?

Try harder of course. I was so desperate for love and acceptance that I became demanding in my pursuit of it. Oh, and I blamed—a lot, and in the process my ego would validate and support me. "He didn't respect me." "He treated me unfairly." And the big one—"he didn't know how to love!" Oh, the naïve arrogance of me not recognizing that I too didn't know how to love. The wall I had built to protect myself wasn't just bricks and mortar. I'd built a fortress of steel around my heart the likes of which would rival Fort Knox.

I could no longer stay in a barren marriage where neither of us really knew how to love, let alone how to make it great. But I agonized over leaving. Every night as I watched my daughters sleep, I felt guilty about separating them from their dad. So I stayed. The final nail in the coffin of my marriage came from my dad. His argument for why I should "tough it out" was that my husband was a "good provider." This reasoning had the opposite affect of what was intended. I was suffering with depression and no amount of money would provide the nourishment my soul needed. Leaving was the only option because we didn't deserve an unhappy life.

I made a vow to myself that I would never be lonely and feel unloved in a relationship again. It was time for me to take charge of my life, find self-worth, and live with passion. After hearing my declaration, a friend bought me a copy of Marianne Williamson's, *A Woman's Worth*. I loved her views on all aspects of being female, especially how she wove spirituality and sexuality together. I was hooked.

A few years, a few men, and many books and courses later, I met my new husband-to-be. He rode in on a white stallion and I fell instantly in love…well, not exactly. I was leery. My track record wasn't stellar and I trusted my kids' intuition more than my own so I asked their opinion. Their approval was the beginning of my new romance that was nothing short of passionate. I was feeling really good about myself and life. I'd done a lot of personal development, was on track toward a degree in human sexuality, I was laughing—a lot. I'd stepped through the cage door of depression. I was flying high in this new relationship. Until I wasn't.

Ever so slowly we started sliding into patterns that left us feeling unloved and not cared for. I could see us drifting apart and in panicked desperation guess what I did? I stepped right back into my old shit of blame and demand, causing him to withdraw, me to push harder and him to pull further away. I was devastated. "How was it possible that I was right back where I vowed I would never be again—lonely in a relationship?" We had become toxic and at times volatile, and I was grieving the love I had found and then unconsciously lost. As stress mounted and trust and safety eroded, our downward spiral picked up speed. We were going down in flames and there was nothing I could do.

I was back in the cage of depression, my husband was diagnosed with type II diabetes and our sex life flatlined. We were dying from the inside out. Life didn't feel worth living because I couldn't escape the reality that the common denominator in my failed attempts at finding true love was me. I believed I didn't matter, wasn't good enough, was unlovable and powerless to change it. Imagine a very thin fragile glass container with a tornado of sharp rocks swirling inside. That was how I experienced the excruciating combination of anxiety and depression. I didn't even care that the antidepressants weren't working. I started planning for the end of my life.

Looking up at the hotel where I was going to put an end to my intense grief I felt completely numb. I don't know how long I was frozen in place before I heard the voice in my head telling me to go home. I had a vision of my daughters, now grown and living on their own, and I knew I had to listen to the message I was receiving. So began the return to my spiritual and sexual journey. You see, I'd forsaken it a few years back thinking I was all fixed, life was great, and I had learned all I needed. Big, *big* mistake! I was humbled by my arrogance once again with renewed dedication to turn things around and make our love great.

With me leading the charge, we immersed ourselves in counseling, personal growth retreats, and a couple's retreat. We were digging haphazardly into what caused all our trouble with no real direction and it felt like we were taking one step forward then another back. During this whole chaotic time I was feeling like a complete fraud in my work, *Who the fuck am I to be helping people with their sexuality when my life is such a hot mess?* I wondered. I was fiercely determined to find answers, solutions, something, *anything* that would get us back to rainbows and orgasms!

I started reading and studying everything I could get my hands on and my clients provided a valuable clue. They were coming to me with sexual concerns but I saw that almost 100% of their troubles were because of intimacy problems that weren't physical. Ah-ha! Intimacy is where all the baggage is! So I dove headfirst into researching intimacy. The romance I craved was coming back during our weekends away but trust was slow to grow because we were still protecting our hearts. It disturbed me that I was waffling back and forth between feeling hopeful yet still dancing with the thought of divorce, so I forced myself to question and dissect every thought I had and emotion I felt.

I was learning to face my shit and own it. I was even off the antidepressants. Instead of playing small like I had my whole life I was starting to joyfully embrace my authentic self, stand in my power, and ever so slightly I started to believe in a glimmering hope that there were immense possibilities waiting for me. My gut told me I would find the key to my own peace and happiness. My mind told me nothing would change unless we were both fully in.

It was time to piss or get off the pot.

I challenged my husband with something like, "If we're going to go the distance. If we're going to make it we have to both be fully committed. And it can't be living here where so much sorrow, anger and loneliness has ruled our existence. I need to get out before depression swallows me whole. I need to leave this place and all the negative influences behind." (And trust me—there were a lot!)

He agreed and I felt an overwhelming flood of relief. He was willing to join me. So we sold our house and most everything in it, and hit the road with no plan. I didn't care where we were going. I just needed to get the hell outta Dodge. But there was one thing I needed to do before we left. I wrote a letter to God. I needed *all* the help I could get.

Dear God,

I want to live where I will wake up feeling happy, loved and accepted.

I want to live where I will prosper financially and thrive physically, mentally, emotionally and spiritually.

I want to live where I will be creative, inspired and energetic.

I want to live where my gifts will be nurtured and my divine radiance can shine bright.

Please help me be open to the signs and fearless in following them.

Thank you for the abundance I already have and all that has yet to be.

Love,

Gayle

With every mile we traveled, and every fragment of negative energy left behind, I felt lighter and I could breathe easier. I kept telling myself we were running *to* a new lease on life but the voice in my head cautioned that we were also running away and trouble could follow. On one hand life was easier and we were growing together but on the other, healing our relationship wounds along with our childhood wounds was hard, because now we only had each other. We'd left everything and everyone behind, and like it or not we were stuck with each other 24/7.

We settled into a new home on the other side of the country and life was looking up. We were implementing everything I was developing in my work. I no longer felt like a fraud because I was practicing what I preached and we were tuning into each other intimately. I could taste freedom. I wasn't in the cage anymore. I was on the outside but I was still tethered and frustrated. There was still something holding me back from being able to fly but I couldn't put my finger on it.

And then it hit. The emotional storm that almost ended us. The monster fight that lasted until the wee hours of the morning. I don't even remember how it started but I was back in blame, anger, and hurt mode, and I was scared that things were never really going to change. So I left.

I knew with every fiber of my being that I was being tested and I had to face my shit—*again!* I could feel the familiar whisper of depression, shame, and defeat trying to coax me back to not worthy, not good enough, unaccepted, unloved, and abandoned.

It was 5:00 AM. With tears streaming down my face I finally got tired of my own bullshit. In the lonely predawn hotel room I wrote an email to a spiritual coach I'd been following and said that I needed serious help and how soon could we start work. It took every ounce of strength I had left to click send.

The next day with our tails between our legs, my husband and renewed our commitment to us. Less than a week after that I met my new coach, spilled my story and was asked, "If you don't stay together what's the worst thing that could happen?" I was shocked that the only answer I had was, "nothing." I knew in that instant that something substantial had shifted inside me. My rock bottom moment was in the past. I'd already experienced the worst case scenario—and survived.

Through the work I did with my coach I finally let go of the limiting beliefs I had lived with for years on end. I dug deeper on my own and released the trauma I had carried through life. I completely let go of all the old hurts by learning how to truly forgive others, and more importantly myself. Without the need to protect my heart, the cord that tethered me to the cage vanished. I now realize, I had created the cage that I held myself captive in. It wasn't long after that I discovered the letter I had written to God so long ago. In hindsight I could see all the clues the Universe provided that guided me to where I am now. This time my tears were filled with joy.

I fully learned to love who I truly am.

My husband followed my lead and started doing his own deeper work. It only takes one person to start to change the dynamic of a relationship. I love the passion, fun and flow we now have in love, intimacy, and sex. Yes, we still have moments of disconnection, times when we're careless with our thoughts, words, or actions—last I checked we're still human—but we get through those times. I'm at peace knowing that no matter what, I have everything I need within me—body, mind, heart, and spirit.

I've had a lot of great teachers along the way sharing the benefits of self-love. Yet, no one mentioned that to get to the deep love that leads to peace you have to be willing to embrace intimacy. There's a reason my tagline is "Intimacy is the gateway to great sex and love!" There's no way around it. Intimately connecting with a partner in life begins by intimately knowing yourself first.

Now, my work is more fulfilling than ever. The success my clients are having is deeply moving. Some of them start off skeptical but they all make leaps and bounds forward, surprising themselves, but not me.

Your journey doesn't need to be as difficult as mine. You have the power to create a life that lights you up the way mine does for me. You just need to know how. And that's where I come in.

Email me at gayle@drgaylefriend.com and together let's make love great.

About the Author

Gayle Friend is a doctor of human sexuality. Intimacy expert. Keynote speaker, author, science, sex, and spiritual geek. And a love junkie. She's internationally known for her success in helping people to increase passion and pleasure, enjoy close emotional intimacy, and communicate openly with ease. Dr. Gayle's approach is different from traditional talk therapy. She combines all of her passions and many modalities that empower her clients to make leaps and bounds in their lives. She works with individuals, couples, and corporations who value happy, healthy relationships. If you're ready to live in peace and harmony, you're in the perfect place at the perfect time!

Join her Make Love Great community:
www.DrGayleFriend.com/makelovegreatgroup

Request a gift session with Dr. Gayle:
www.makelovegreat.com/giftcall

The Miracle of Obstacles

Evakarin Wallin

In the late eighties I was living in Östersund, a small town in Sweden and working long hours every day, until my first daughter was six months old. Her father and I owned a popular store downtown where we sold clothing and jewelry. We also had a small factory where we made knit sweaters. Our business was going well. It was the economic boom time of the eighties, and everyone had disposable income. But not long after this, we were hit with a recession and sales stopped. We were not prepared and our business went bankrupt. Thank God for that.

If that had not happened I would probably have not slowed down, not spent enough time with my baby daughter, or with myself. But I didn't know that then. For two months after we went bankrupt, I was climbing the walls in our home. I was stressed about not working and helping to provide for our needs. Only taking care of the family was not enough to make me feel good—useful, like I was contributing. I didn't understand it then, but looking back now, it was obvious.

That period marks the start of my personal journey. A journey to myself, and to a life that not only sustained me emotionally but also spiritually and financially. Was it painful? Yes, but also necessary. If we are not challenged, we do not grow. If we do not feel the pain of change, we will never fulfill our potential. Too often we go through the motions. It's so easy to live an okay life and not listen to the message coming from within us. This message that tells us we can do what aligns with our spirit and live a life that fulfills us and *also* helps others. I am grateful now for the pain I went through. It made me become the person I was meant to be.

But it was not an easy start for me. Until then life had just happened to me. And I can remember thinking: How did I end up here? And here was not a pretty place. The relationship I was in was not very supportive. And still, he was the man pointing me in the direction of personal growth.

After the bankruptcy I became an avid learner in personal development and spirituality. The first book read was *Creative Visualization* by Shakti Gawain. I was both skeptical and curious at the same time. I couldn't figure out how, by changing my thoughts, I could change my life. Thoughts are made of nothing and the world is very physical, I thought. At the same time if this really was true I did not want to miss out. Though I was skeptical, I started to make positive affirmations.

When I was eight months pregnant with my second child I had enough of the relationship. I just took my then two-year-old daughter in my hand and walked out with no plan or place to go. In the town I lived in there was always a shortage of places to rent. So if I had been planning to leave it would have taken a long time for me to get a place for us. Although I was homeless, for the first time in a long time, I felt happy and free.

Then a miracle happened. It only took me two weeks to find and move into our new apartment. Was it the affirmations that did it? I was still doubtful.

My ex-husband was not happy with me leaving. He tried different things to make me come back. A year after we had separated when I was bringing the children to visit him as I often did, he threatened me to move back in with him. If I did not promise he would not let me leave. I felt I had no choice but to promise. But I said I would do it in five months.

Not long after, I started to have these crazy dreams about a former boyfriend. We had not seen each other in years but I kept having the dreams so I felt that I had to contact him. I did and we started having a relationship. I knew then that I could not fulfill my promise to go back to the father of my children. One week before I was supposed to move back in with the father of my children, I called him and said I was not coming. His response was: Then I will come and take the children. I had no legal right to stop him. I could do nothing. I decided that if the highest path for them was to live with their father I had to let go. If the highest path for them was to live with me I would be grateful. And then I let go of that too. I did not try to stop him when he came and took the children away.

But it was time to put my spiritual ideas to the test.

I not only did affirmations. I also focused on letting go of my fears and asking for help to accept whatever happened. I took long walks and focused on letting go and praying for my children. Three months went by and my ex called me and said: You can come and take them back whenever you want.

I did not doubt anymore.

My boyfriend and I lived happily together with my two children. And we also had two children together. Then he died suddenly. I was devastated. He had been the love of my life and now he was gone...again. I felt totally lost. But I could not give up. I had four children to care for. So I pulled myself together, I had to be strong. I did not deal with my sorrow. The children had lost their father. That was worse than me losing a partner, I told myself. It worked for a while.

I met someone and started another relationship and a few years later I got pregnant again. But I had not dealt with my past sorrow and I went into a deep depression. On July 23rd in 2001 I gave birth to the sweetest baby girl. I am so grateful for her and for all of my children. But I was still depressed. During this time I met

Sylvi from Denver Colorado. She was a life coach visiting friends in Sweden. Although I didn't't really know what coaching was I knew intuitively that it was also my path. I hired Sylvi as my coach and she inspired me to go to Chicago for a coaching conference. I took her advice and I loved everything about the experience, which was so was positive and uplifting.

I started my coaching training the same year and it changed my life. But there were many other changes happening during that time, some quite unforeseen. My partner and I separated and I became a single mom with now, five children. I was on my own. This was one of the most stressful times of my life. For five years there was never enough money. I was always late paying the bills, and I never knew if I would be able to pay my yearly taxes on time. I was exhausted and all my childhood issues; feelings of not being good enough, were haunting me.

It is well known that getting a divorce, moving, starting a new relationship, and the death of a loved one, are the biggest causes of stress. All of that had happened to me during a period of a few short years. Some of them, I had done several times over. And on top of all that I was struggling with money and with providing for my family. No wonder I felt worn out I *was* worn out. But there was no time to rest, I had to keep going. My children were depending on me. *I* was depending on me.

My lowest point was when I had to sell my house. I had lost my company due to unpaid taxes. Which made it hard to rent an apartment. The money I received from selling the house I had to split with my ex-partner, so it was not enough for me to buy something else. I was lost. I didn't know what to do. Every morning when I woke up, I would feel good for a moment, and then it would hit me. *Where are we going to live?* That realization brought back the weight of all the burdens and responsibilities I was carrying. If it were only me I could have slept on a friend's sofa, but I had five children. I was overwhelmed; the anxiety and panic immobilized me. If I couldn't find a place to live, how could I take care of my children? I was in a dark place. I didn't know where to turn. I gave up.

I stopped struggling and looking for answers outside of myself. Instead, I took long walks in the forest. I walked for at least two hours a day wherever my feet took me. My only focus was to release the tension I had inside me. After a few weeks, my stress decreased. I started to feel confident and to trust in myself. One afternoon I was out for my usual long walk, but that day I decided to take a different route. I was on the outskirts of town just outside the forest when I saw a house. It didn't look like anyone lived there because the garden was unkempt and the grass had grown very high, so I peeked inside the window. It was empty.

I was excited as I hurried back home. I did some research and found out who owned it. I contacted the owners who agreed to rent it to me, and it did not take long until we moved in. It seemed like a great weight was lifted from my shoulders. I felt like I could relax and get back to the work I so loved. But work was a struggle. I was totally stressed out. The only way I could ease my stress was to do more. Looking back I was not very productive. I was running around in circles doing things to ease my stress.

Then I attended a week long course called Masters of Manifestation. I did not have high expectations of it. But that week changed my life completely. Finally I understood why my affirmations seemed to work sometimes but not always. I learned about shadow work. How our beliefs in our subconscious mind keeps create our choices and results in our lives. I went deep into shadow work and suddenly I felt like my life was a piece of clay that I could mold into anything I wanted.

What I have learned is that at times, my emotions run me and subsequently, my life. What is deep inside of me often controls my actions. My fears and insecurities were making choices for me and creating a life that was more about *reacting* and not about *consciously* acting. The patterns I have, mostly from childhood, were making the choices for me. What I can see so clearly now, is that, although I was dearly loved when I was a child, I did not understand it. And because I thought I was unloved, I believed I was unlovable—not worthy of love—and I constantly sought it outside of myself. It was that belief that made me go in to the relationship with the father of my two oldest children. It is neither good nor bad. It was painful but a lot of things that I value came thanks to that. My belief that I was not loved made me end up in situations so I could recognize the limiting belief I had. I felt like life just happened to me. But it was my subconscious pattern that pulled me into different situations. I know now that love starts from within. What the miracle of the obstacles I had to overcome taught me is that it's up to us to create the life we want to live. What I learned over the years is that those uncomfortable feelings and emotions are only information from the subconscious to the conscious mind about a limiting belief that you have about yourself.

This is an exercise in 5 easy steps I feel is very helpful to stop fighting with the uncomfortable feelings and to help them let go of me.

1. **Notice where you feel some kind of stress or unease in your body.** Usually it is somewhere in your body. Put your hand on your chest, solar plexus, or stomach to see if you find any tension there. Just notice it. You don't have to do anything about it.

2. **Listen to what limiting belief you have about yourself that goes together with the feeling.** Many times it is a version of not feeling good enough, fear of being rejected, or unwanted

or that you don't believe you are able to manage a specific situation.

3. **When you become aware of what is going on, can you see what you want instead?** If you feel not good enough. Do you long for feeling that you *are* good enough? If you don't believe that you can manage a specific situation, would you like to feel confident that you *can* manage. Whatever your limiting belief is, it shows you that you long for something different. It helps you to become aware.

4. **Give thanks to the uncomfortable feeling.** It came to you and opened up your awareness. It is a gift and when you treat it like that it will let go of you. It's purpose is not to harm you or to make you feel small. It wants to communicate to you and when you listen it has fulfilled its purpose and will then leave you.

5. **Now wait for inspiration.** When you feel calm and balanced again you will be able to hear your intuition. Because you have released some limiting belief you have changed. And you will do things in a different way. Without even thinking about it. You have cleared something that was standing in the way from you seeing your true self.

If we listen to the message coming from within, we can learn from it, we can grow, and we can be the creator of our best life. Once we understand how to use our feelings and emotions, and harness their intuitive energy, instead of simply reacting to them, we can create positive energy in our life and in the world.

About the Author

Evakarin Wallin is on a mission to create peace on earth by helping people find peace within themselves, and ultimately within their life. She is the founder of Freedom Based Mindset, a technique that has helped hundreds of people to easily and effortlessly release old patterns and limiting beliefs. She helps them to understand how to use their emotions to create flow in life and work. Her journey has taught her that true freedom is when you are not controlled by your emotions, when they don't run you, or dictate your actions. To be free is to act on your emotions and not react to them.

Visit www.awakecommunication.com

The Voice Within

Joana Soares

My name is Joana and I'm a dreamer. My main goal in life is finding my purpose and my inner happiness, applying the verb "to help" along the way. I was born in the early nineties into a middle-class family in the marvelous city of Porto, Portugal. I was a happy kid, always talking, asking questions, and telling stories. I was sociable, a good student, and a good friend. During my teens I was diagnosed with obesity (early stage). I began not to like the way I looked and to think I wasn't pretty enough or thin enough. I saw myself as a failure and believed that I wasn't good enough. That's when the problems started.

I would look at myself in the mirror and think I was so far away from the "perfect" body. Every time I ate something that I wasn't supposed to, I had a deep feeling of guilt. I felt like I couldn't go on, that I was disappointing everyone (and myself). One morning while riding my bicycle down the hill, I thought, *What if I rode off the cliff? What if my life ended here? I would finally stop hurting? Would anyone even notice?* Sometimes I would go to the beach to be alone with my thoughts. I would look out at the waves and breathe deeply in and out, to find the strength to go on.

One day, feeling depressed, I ate a lot of chocolate and other "forbidden things" and got so sick that I vomited. The feeling of lightness afterward was a relief. The thought that I could eat what I wanted then get rid of it, made me bulimic before I even knew what the disease was. This went on for months. Although I was sick and not feeling well from vomiting, a lot of people told me how pretty and skinny I was. Their appreciation fueled my new habit and kept me purging in secret.

My parents saw I was losing weight but didn't know how I was doing it. They discovered my problem because I'd circled an article in a magazine about bulimia. This upset them and they started to "chase me." They would follow me to the bathroom after I ate, and they became very controlling. Although I knew they were trying to help, it was a very distressing and embarrassing time in my life. I wanted to lose weight but dieting and exercise hadn't helped. The only thing that did was purging. But I could see how it was affecting my parents and also my body and health. I knew it couldn't continue. After attending a conference on bulimia and eating disorders, my parents better understood the disease and they searched for someone to help me. They found a wonderful psychologist who helped me understand my self-esteem issues, and made me believe in myself again by drawing out my strengths, and appreciating me and praising me for my intrinsic qualities—my outgoing personality and my natural talents (to be persistent, passionate, affectionate, honest, an eternal student, and my ability to make people feel better and inspired).

She introduced me to the book *Wokini: A Lakota Journey to Happiness and Self-Understanding by Nicholas Sparks and Billy Mills*, the Portuguese version is titled *Uma Viagem Espiritual*. From it I learned the life-changing lesson that happiness comes from within. This new insight helped me to beat bulimia. I started to work on myself—from the inside out—and to focus on a different subject: my studies.

In 2008 I entered veterinary school and discovered my PASSION. I have always loved animals. When I was ten years old my dream was to have a dog. I told a friend of my parents and she gave me a black Cocker Spaniel puppy. The first dream of my life was realized when I met Lucky, who became my best friend.

I was doing well at university. I loved anatomy, the medical disciplines, the skills that I needed to develop to make a diagnosis and to help the animals in need. During my first year at the end of the second semester, despite all my hard work, I failed four disciplines. I was devastated, exhausted, overwhelmed, and sad. But I was not alone. Some of my friends had the same problem, we worked hard but we didn't always pass our exams.

During a school holiday, I went on a trip with my family and I forgot the university, the classes, and the exams. When I was to return to school my sister made me a poster that read: You can do it! I'm an animal in need and I need you! You are the best veterinarian in the world.

I was so grateful for her thoughtfulness. Those words helped me a lot. Whenever I felt defeated at school I'd read the poster and it gave me strength. During that time I found out that I was inherently strong and had all the qualities I needed to overcome, already inside me. I just had to acknowledge them and draw on them. I learned that I was persistent and courageous. I had strength of will, a thirst for knowledge; and the ability to overcome obstacles and to transform them into lessons. My time at university brought me another family; the faculty became my support group and also my friends. We'd often get together over meals to share experiences, traditions, and stories. Knowing that they were there for me, gave me strength.

One night, after yet another magnificent dinner with my university family, a friend asked if I had considered studying for a year abroad in Brazil. I hadn't thought about it. I'd been in Northeastern Brazil in 2004 with my family and I had fallen in love with the people, the diverse culture, and the gorgeous landscape. I was excited about returning to that wonderful place and spending a year there. I was overjoyed when my parents said I could study abroad. This incident taught me courage and to ask for what I want. If I hadn't believed in the possibility of going to Brazil and asked my parents they would not have surprised me by allowing me to go.

I spent 2011 in Brazil. During that time I learned that there are a lot of people like me: talkative, cheerful, sociable, friendly, and curious. I also learned the importance of patience and that we can be happy, no matter what we have in our lives. I learned how important it is to see the joy in little moments. I also discovered my spiritual side and came to understand that gratitude and love are always the right path.

I left Brazil almost a new person and when I returned to university I found Louis the love of my life, again. Louis and I were going through growing pains and broke up before I left for Brazil. When I returned, I had much more awareness of myself and of life and I fell deeply in love with him again. He really is a wonderful guy, he understands me—sometimes better than I understand myself—and he showed me how to appreciate simplicity.

In 2014, my beloved dog Lucky, became sick and it felt like my world had collapsed. There I was, a veterinary student, almost a doctor, and I couldn't help him. For a long time I knew he was not doing well, but my parents and my teacher (his doctor) didn't believe me. During a consultation I asked the vet if Lucky had Leishmaniosis, a very common disease in Coimbra, in the center of Portugal (where we have a house and where Lucky was living most of the weekends). His vet dismissed the question because, the symptoms didn't match. A week later, Lucky underwent surgery to remove a mass and we discovered he had Lymphoma and Leishmaniosis. He was very sick and getting sicker. My family and I stayed with him until the end. We are grateful to a teacher who helped us to understand his problem so we could better face the pain.

When Lucky died I lost my best friend. His death taught me some important lessons: to be grateful for the present moment, and to enjoy every day as if it were your last. I also learned that life doesn't mean anything without the people we love.

When I finished my studies and became a vet, I considered moving to Brazil where I'd had the best year of my life, or to France because of the excellent opportunities there for my profession. But the universe had other plans for me. My grandmother Rose (whom I love dearly) was diagnosed with a skin tumor. At that same time, my sister was diagnosed with an ovarian tumor. My decision was made for me. I decided to stay in Portugal to be close to them.

Thankfully, the tumors were benign, and they were both fine. The blessings didn't end there. I had many job opportunities in Portugal the best ones were total opposites: a small clinic in Porto, near my family or a hospital in the south of Portugal, 600 km away in Algarve. My heart told me to go to Algarve. It was the right choice. Louis and I moved there and he found a job. I loved working at the hospital and living with Louis. I was good with my clients and the animals, and I had a wonderful working relationship with my coworkers, and the team.

As a vet, my best quality was that I cared deeply. When I was giving a traumatic diagnosis, I put myself in the owner's position (like I had been with Lucky) and I tried to be that comforting presence and the doctor Lucky and I didn't have when he was sick. I made an effort to understand their concerns and fears and to treat the animals with compassion and respect.

I strove to be the best employee I could be. So I took on a lot of extra shifts, and helped out whenever it was needed (Sundays, nights, holidays) and became "the glue" that held our team together. But I wasn't taking care of myself. I started to have health problems because my immune system was low. It was at this point that I began to feel undervalued for all the time and energy I was putting in at the hospital. I was stressed out and anxious and it was affecting my relationship with Louis. I had to reevaluate. Here I was living in a beautiful city near the beach, but I rarely went there because I worked so much. I was also far away from my family and my friends. Deep down I knew that, because of this lack of balance, my health would suffer.

In 2016 I discovered the book *The Secret* and the karmic Law of Attraction and I knew in my heart it was the reason why my life had seemed so dark in the past. I was attracting things I didn't want because I was always thinking about them. After that, I paid close attention to my thoughts, to my intuition, and to "the voice within." That's when I realized that thinking positively and practicing positive values like love, tenderness, peace, joy, and hope, would be my new way of life. I now understood that we ARE our daily thoughts and our emotions and that "Energy goes where energy flows." I'd felt it in Brazil, I only needed to remember it. During my consultations, it became even clearer. Sometimes a sick dog or cat came from a family that was also sick—with health problems, low energy, and sometimes even with the same disease. During our thirty minutes of consultation I tried to have—and to give—the best energy I could. I also gave myself that same positive energy.

This was why I didn't break down in the middle of the hospital chaos and long and intense work hours. An old (forgotten) passion of mine also helped me through those tough times. When I was a kid I read tons of books and I loved it! Encouraged by what I'd learned in *The Secret* I started to read more. It was amazing, like a breath of fresh air! I also spent more time in nature, and enjoying every free moment I had with Louis, by going for long walks near the river, the mountains, or the ocean.

In 2017, when I was reading the book *Free Yourself From Toxic Thoughts* by Rute Caldeira, I completed The Wheel of Life exercise, in which you create a wheel and color the different parts of your life—for instance career, love, wealth, health—to show how you value its different aspects. Doing this showed me that my lowest value was career. I had been going through the motions for a while, but now I knew I had to do something if I wanted to feel whole and be happy. I applied the visualization techniques I'd learned and considered, if I left Algarve where would I go? Then I paid attention to what the universe sent me. Not long after, I opened a veterinary magazine and saw a former professor of mine in a veterinary hospital in Porto, my hometown. I knew then what to do. I applied for a position at the hospital and a month later I was heading home to Porto for an interview! Guess what happened next? I was chosen for the job!

There is a saying: Be careful what you wish for because you just might get it. I was now faced with making a choice. Do I risk everything I had accomplished in Algarve—which was no longer making me happy—to start over in Porto? I meditated about it and one day at the beach that little voice said, "It's time to change!" And that voice deep down inside me, was right. We know intrinsically when our situation no longer suits us, makes us unhappy, or unhealthy. But it's up to us to ask the right questions of the universe and then be willing, and brave enough to make a change.

Now here I am, redefining my dreams. After I made that change, I was invited to participate in this book and I thought: *I have to try, maybe it's the right path for another passion of mine—writing. Maybe this is my opportunity to once again, apply the verb, "to help" with my words, and to heal myself and my demons along the way.*

My name is Joana. Nice to meet you.

About the Author

Joana Soares is a passionate veterinarian from Porto, Portugal. She works in a veterinary hospital and cares deeply about her patient's well being as well as their owner's concerns and feelings. She is a dreamer and wishes she could help the world to see animals as lovable sentient beings, and thinks the solution is education. Joana hopes her story will inspire and help people and make them believe that anything is possible. She believes that love is the answer to all and she has a strong will to help people and animals all over the world.

To find out more and talk with Joana please write to: youarenotalonejoana@gmail.com

How Could I be Stressed? I'm an Olympic Athlete!

Jesper Pilegaard

I have always thought I could handle a lot of pressure—and I can. But you can be in a situation where you don't know that you are in funnel—where the pressure increases exponentially and you don't feel its effects until it's almost too late.

I know. I've been there!

This is My Story

I worked in a bank for more than thirty years. I was also a successful key account manager for over twenty years. I'm the type of man who never gets tired, I could work like ten horses, and was used to working and competing while under intense pressure. I got this from being an Olympian. What I didn't expect was how my work ethic almost worked against me.

I had been working with a customer/vendor for some years. It wasn't a success in the beginning, but we discovered that if we were more flexible, we could increase our business. In the next few years we had a flourishing partnership. It was the beginning of a great working relationship. After four years with that customer, my manager asked me to take over another manufacturer, MANU, and their importer, VEND. The bank had tried to put together a partnership with them for three years, with three different key account managers. I had 24 hours to make my decision! A colleague said that the partnership would never work. We'd already been trying for three years! But if I wasn't successful, everyone at the bank would understand. I decided to accept the challenge.

I'm a Fighter—I'm a Winner

In the beginning, I was placed at VEND three to four days a week, to show our good intentions. I participated in nearly all their internal sales meetings. But there was a long way to go. Both the management team at the bank and at VEND were committed in the beginning, at least *officially*. But when it came to action and daily work there was no real commitment. They left it to me to make it happen. It was very frustrating that the top management in the bank didn't support me. Because of it the initial sales figures were bad. But my manager knew the situation and told me, "Don't worry. I know the case and you're doing a good job, the management team at VEND says that too." After a year, I was even given a $4,000 raise in salary.

Unfortunately the salesmen at VEND were not being cooperative. The were unhappy with the agreement that VEND had signed and did everything to work against it. I worked many hours for VEND, much more than was expected, but the salesmen were still dissatisfied. They would call me at all hours from early morning to late at night, any day of the week, and they expected me to drop what I was doing and respond immediately.

As an Olympian, I have always set goals and milestones in order to achieve my targets and it was completely incomprehensible to me that the salesmen would oppose the goal set by their management. I was measured by MANU by how many of their machines were financed at VEND. And I was criticized for sales being below expectations. Still, my closest manager was behind me. But I still felt a lot of pressure because the partnership and sales figures didn't show an increase.

After working long hours with VEND for nearly three years, suddenly my manager in the bank, his manager, and our CEO were fired due to changes in our organization. We would not have replacements for six months. I now had no one to turn to for support. It didn't take long before the salesmen at VEND discovered that I no longer had backup at the bank. Now when I went to sales meetings at VEND, the sales management did everything to undermine me. I'm at fighter—and I fought very hard. I worked long hours. I was at the beck and call of the salesforce. I put my needs, and even my health, on the back burner to make the partnership a success. During that tine I had no idea how the constant underlying stress and the toxic work environment was affecting me.

A New Manager

Six months later, I got a new manager. I talked to him about the case and he was supportive and wanted to make the partnership a success. For the next three months I used the qualities I have as an Olympian—to worked like ten horses, I was supportive and a team player—to come up with creative solutions and campaigns for VEND. Their management team thought we were going in the right direction. But their salesmen were still uncooperative.

At the end of the year it was time for an internal evaluation of the cooperation in the bank. We concluded that we needed a new commitment from VEND. We had at big meeting with representatives from MANU, VEND and the bank, coming from USA, Europe, and Scandinavia. We made a new plan and agreed that we would increase our commitment to the written agreement we had signed four years ago.

My manager asked me to make a new strategy. I did and when I presented it to him, he said it wasn't good enough. He said I should forget about what had happened in the past and look forward. I made a new plan that we introduced to VEND's management team. It was a total failure.

Knocked Down

I was knocked down mentally, emotionally, and physically. I was now feeling the effects of how hard I'd been working for the last year. I was at my wit's end and close to a breakdown. When I got home my wife Lene, saw how upset I was. She told me, "STOP, you'll make yourself sick if you continue like this. You need a break *now*! If you don't stop, you'll end up in the hospital." She then ordered me to go to the doctor.

I asked for two more days at work, so I could finish up some work, and then I would go to the doctor. She accepted that. As promised, I went to see my doctor two days later. After examining me he demanded that I stop working, *immediately* if I wanted to stay alive! I was on the verge of a mental and physical collapse. I was totally stressed and exhausted. I needed a break—NOW!

What Should I Do?

I went home in shock, wondering *what should I do?* Should I listen to the doctor's orders to stay home, to stop working, and to catch up on my exercise and rest? Exercising wouldn't be a problem. I loved playing badminton, as well as sailing and cycling. But as a former Olympian, it was—and still is—difficult not to exercise without being competitive. This is not good for a stressed body. If you push your body too hard, you will stress it. But a walk in the park was not much fun for me. Lene came up with a solution. She gave me a pedometer so I could see how much I had walked during the day. My goal for each day was 11,000 steps. At first, it took me a few days to reach it. After that, my goal was to see how many days in a row I could walk 11,000 steps. It was a good start, but only working on my body was not enough. I also needed to work on my brain to calm my thoughts. I began to practice mindfulness and yoga. Mindfulness is incredibly calming because it centers you, using it along with Yin Yoga, my brain and body started to recover.

Getting Help

I also started going to a psychologist. In the beginning, it was okay, but after ten sessions I felt as if it was turning more into small talk than therapy. A friend recommended a psychotherapist he had used. Here the chemistry between the therapist and I was much better. She spoke a "language" that I could understand. She also taught me a very simple thing. If you can't do anything about it—"why worry?" After that many things clicked into place. Even when I say it today, it relaxes me.

This perspective was also important when I felt uncomfortable about a situation or felt like I had no control, I'd say, "why worry?" and I'd feel the pressure start to lift. Doing this relieved me of some of the need to control what was happening, put me in a positive frame of mind, and calmed me. It may seem a bit strange, but it worked for me. I also realized that acknowledging and being open about stress was the way out of my stress. It's easy to be aware of a problem, but it's far more difficult to solve it.

How Did I Get Here?

As I was taking my long walks to meet my 11,000 steps I would think about my life and work, and consider the questions my psychotherapist asked me. One was: Why did I get into such a stressful situation?

First, I'm a "pleaser." It's important to me that others are doing well. But very often I put their needs before my own. I often compromised my own values to help others. As my therapist said, Jesper, it's like when you're on a plane. You put the oxygen mask on first *before* helping others! If not, you'll be of no help to anyone. Being a "pleaser" I always helped others before myself. Because of it I often put myself into situations where I was in a huge time crunch and immense pressure. Today, I am much more aware of those situations. I'm not an expert yet, but I am getting better every day.

As a "pleaser" it was important for me to keep my promises and commitments. When others did not keep their part of the agreement, I was incredibly disappointed but I did not often speak up, when it was the manager. I now know how important it is to communicate my feelings. As long as I did so in a positive and constructive way.

Pride

Another big challenge was my pride. As a man and a former Olympian, I was ashamed and embarrassed that I couldn't handle my job and this situation. Pride also kept me from telling my family and friends that I was sick with stress. I was so embarrassed. Of course, Lene and my children knew about it, but no one else did. After long talks with my wife, I accepted that I needed to open up to my family and closest friends about how stress had affected my health. I told first my brother and my wife's parents. They were shocked because I'd always been so strong mentally and physically. But telling them was a great release and they became a support group for me.

A New Passion!

During that time, my wife gave me a notebook to write my thoughts in. I didn't think much about it, but I did it every day. In the beginning, it was just a few words and sentences, but as the time went by, I started writing longer sentences and then paragraphs and it became another kind of therapy. I would write about ideas I had, and problems I wanted to find solutions for. It then became my mission, to find a way of preventing or overcoming stress, through lectures and coaching. It gave me a new passion for life and a new direction!

Now that I'd told my family the next step was to tell my friends. That was very difficult. When I told it to a friend the first time, I said it very quickly, "By the way, I've been on sick leave for stress for two months. How are your children doing?" I was hoping he would answer the question and not ask about my illness. But that's not what happened. Instead he asked me about it in the very best way. His concern for me made it a little easier to talk about it and to tell other friends. Their reaction was always supportive and positive. It was a big relief to tell others about my sickness. My friends respected that I was doing something about and was willing to talk openly about it.

As I told more of my friends, it became easier. Women often told me how admirable it was that as a man I was open about it and wasn't afraid to be vulnerable. Suddenly, it was my vulnerability that gave me strength, and gave me pride. Soon after, friends and colleagues came to me with questions about stress. It became clear that stress was a taboo topic, especially for men. However, the best way to prevent stress is by being open and taking about it. Quite often, simply talking about stress is a great stress reliever.

Putting Myself First

I was on sick leave for four months. When I returned to work it was terrifying, like when you start a new job. I made a plan for my return together with my doctor and wife. I started working four hours on Monday, Tuesday, Thursday, and Friday. On Wednesdays, I stayed home. Slowly increasing with one hour more a day each week. When I came up to normal time four days a week, I started working half-time on Wednesday and slowly increased it to full time. It took nearly two months to get back to working full time. But it was the right thing to do. I was now putting myself first. I was putting on my oxygen mask so I could do my best work but also take care of myself and be there for my family.

How Should We Handle Stress?

There is no blanket solution for stress, because it's too complex and situational. But an early diagnosis and an open dialogue about stress will certainly reduce how it affects us and subsequently our loved ones. If we are more open about our stress and we dare to be vulnerable and honest, we can get help, foster awareness, and minimize its harmful effects. Personally, I believe that taking care of yourself first, is always the right path to well being, and will influence the outcome of all your endeavors for the better. If you find yourself stressed, get help. Speak to your family and then a professional who "speaks your language" and is able to communicate with you in a way you can understand. Then come up with a plan of action, be it, exercise, mindfulness, meditation, yoga, long walks, cutting back at work, or setting up boundaries. Find what works for you and stick to it. You deserve it.

About the Author

Jesper Pilegaard was born on March 6, 1964, in Elsinore, Denmark. He worked in banking for thirty years and is a financial advisor and a Key Account Manager. Jesper is a top athlete, a coach and a lecturer. Co-author of the book Time to Rise Jesper holds lectures, and coaches about stress, and "the will to win." Jesper participated in the Olympic Games, and many European and World championships in sailing (470 and Laser). He coaches elite sailors in technique and tactics. Jesper is married to Lene and together they have two children—Cathrine and Gustav. His hobbies are sailing, badminton and cycling. Jesper speaks Danish and English.

Contact information:
www.jesperpilegaard.dk
Email: jesper.pilegaard@olympian.org
Mobile: +45 6056 1020

A Recalcitrant Awakens

Roméo Cournal

Three years ago, I was in one of the most exciting periods of my life. I received official authorization from my employer to leave and set up a business. I was working in Parisian show business. I was friends with and respected by a lot of well-known people from television, cinema, performing arts. I was also coaching top athletes and politicians. I was often invited to prestigious parties that many would have paid dearly to attend. In the long run, I did not even go to many of them. My company was growing more and more, so I decided to settle in the West Indies under the warm blue sky of the Caribbean while my employees worked for me in cold, grey Paris. I was satisfied with just a few local customers, and I was living one of the most thrilling love stories ever. I really thought that I was about to achieve my life purpose, or at least my ideal lifestyle.

Suddenly, in the span of just a few days, everything turned upside down. Until now, I have never understood what really happened, nor how, nor why. My company was in great jeopardy and, more importantly, my wonderful love story fell apart overnight. It was miraculous, but not in the usual positive sense—this was the work of something bigger. It was so weird, but I immediately understood that each catastrophe had a meaning.

I found myself obliged to go back to Paris and consider resuming my old job though I had sworn that I would never again be an employee. I had worked too hard to regress in that way. I didn't want to take a step backward in life. It would be like turning my back on myself and everything I had worked so hard to achieve. At the same time, all the resources I once had were now unavailable to me.

Every night and every day, I wondered: Do I have to find help to decide, or do I have to decide to find help? I asked this question to my peers, my coaches, my friends, my family, but no one could give me a satisfying answer. Voices in my head constantly reminded me that I had children, loans to pay, an apartment, a car, and so many more responsibilities. I was in a frightful dilemma but nothing convinced me to take the risk of being my authentic self.

So, I decided to play it safe and go back to work—and this is where everything took a turn for the worse.

In addition to the shame that I felt deep inside of me, I had to face the reaction of my former office colleagues who felt that I was no longer part of their world. I was now an outsider. People who drive a Mercedes were not allowed in this suffering group of workers. Even the boss didn't have a luxury car. My way of dressing was too elaborate; clients might think I was a senior executive with the power of decision.

Every day I felt more and more sclerotic. I was doing a job that allowed me to pay my bills and maintain my standard of living, but I was so annoyed. Between unnecessary meetings and managerial mistakes that a first-year student would never have made, I no longer had the time or mental energy to ensure the survival of my company and find efficient solutions to straighten out my business. In the evenings, I was teaching my students the exact opposite of what my hierarchical superiors were doing each morning, but there was no one to prevent their mistakes or correct them. I was evolving in an institution where common sense was a professional mistake and where docility was preferred to performance. And I was very efficient...

This is where I met my new girlfriend. Aline was working in the same service, so we had to hide our relationship. At first, she was like an oasis in the desert—but I did not have to disclose that I was drinking from the water of this fountain.

One month later, I had my first anxiety attack in the office. It was my boss who drove me to the emergency room. After one week of sick leave and wondering if I had to take the risk of devoting myself entirely to my business, I chose to return to work. I must say that the insistence of Aline was the driving force behind that decision.

Three weeks later, I had a second anxiety attack at home. This time it was my girlfriend who accompanied me to the hospital emergency room. I began to seriously feel that she was not really supporting me and I was not totally respecting myself. Despite everything in my gut telling me to take a chance on my business, after this second sick leave, I went back to work.

Three weeks later, at the end of what was my worst day at work ever, I had another panic attack at the office. This final time, it was the firemen who took me to the hospital. I have never been back to that office since. A few weeks later, the occupational medicine department declared me unfit to work.

In fact, it was what I wanted. I wanted to quit that job to have time to take care of my business. But I wanted to be able to ensure the security of my daily life. I had already tried to negotiate my dismissal, which would have enabled me to be granted unemployment benefits, but my employer refused to fire me three times!

The only solution I could see on my radar was to lose my health, to demonstrate how poor I was and finally be recognized and supported. Of course, it did not work. It is not until I wrote those words that realized that it's a lesson I'm proud to know now.

Three months after my return to Paris, I had time to manage my business and enough money to live while waiting on my severance payment. But things were not any better. I had lost a lot of energy and was struggling to regain my health. Business had resumed but not enough to avoid the closure of the company at the end of the year. I immediately started another company, but Aline's desire for security was stronger than my desire for freedom. In addition to this, some of my opinions about couple life, politics, and other things were too discordant for her to allow me to express them. My obstinacy about becoming an entrepreneur eventually broke our relationship.

To top it off, phlebitis prevented me from spending Christmas with my children in the West Indies. I was so bad that, at bedtime, I often thought I would not wake up the next morning. In the long run, I resigned myself to death. Provided I do not suffer!

In this crossing of the desert, I kept on searching for an oasis outside of myself. Despite meditation, despite yoga, despite personal development and my spiritual quest, I sought for and I claimed a savior. The only one I found was… Aline. She was my only source of stability, I relied on her so much that I succumbed. She could not stand being broken up and I really need a shoulder to lean on. "At least I'm not alone," I thought. And it's better to be two in case of an emergency. However, my inexplicable splitting headaches didn't cease and another panic attack occurred. In my pursuit of the cause, I became extremely sensitive to the weather and decided to return at home to the West Indies. Aline wasn't in agreement about that, but it was the essential prerequisite for the continuation of our relationship. Two days after landing at Fort-de-France, right at the beginning of summer holidays, I eventually got my breach of contract document. My expected "golden parachute." On this same day, I had a stupid spill. I fell and seriously hurt my knee and had to be hospitalized for two months.

It's very hard to be immobilized for two months when globetrotting is in your DNA. I learned what crying from pain is, and I reached the point where suicide seemed to be the best way out. Then, it started to feel like the only solution. I experienced disappointment from friends that I was counting on, as some of them often disappeared when I needed them.

Aline also didn't travel to support me. One of my favorite singers sang, "Don't let the sun go down on me," but in my case, the night was already very deep and dark. I faced the creeping fear of loneliness until I finally learned that it couldn't, wouldn't, and didn't want to kill me. I reached a breaking point and found myself yearning to go back to Paris. A part of my entourage had defected, those who remained accused the other group of friends to have abandoned me. So few around me seemed to be supportive. At this point, I still did not understand that I needed to find the support from deep inside. Back in Paris, I had a check-up on my knee. I was told that I had a pulmonary embolism. I have never been so close to death; however, I had not seen it coming. Besides, I did not feel any physical pain during the week that I was hospitalized. I had just learned not to be afraid of death because it may not knock on the door, and it may not be scary or sorrowful.

As I had time and wasn't suffering, I took the opportunity to read those books I had promised myself I would read. I watched the videos that I had never made time to watch, and those I wasn't ready to understand. Here came the switch.

I began to experience a totally different state of being—a different level of consciousness. I realized that curing my social self was not healing my true self. I became aware that, from the very beginning, I was hiding my inner sorrow behind confidence or regret. Sometimes one, sometimes the other. I knew that from the perspective of my social self, people who are allies could also be enemies of my authentic self. Situations that feel uncomfortable may be great opportunities for my personal development. I began to understand that what I was looking for was a sense of purpose, and that sense of purpose was driving me inevitably to meet my true self—the one I had never known before.

So, I decided to leave Paris and its broad spectrum of grays. I settled in a new town and was finally feeling good deep inside. I was going crazy searching for a solution to present to a real estate agent until I remembered what happened the year before. I applied my lesson of taking a leap, even before the ground before me appeared, and took the formal decision to move to Nice, in the South of France, no matter what it took.

Finding an apartment when you are jobless and you walk with crutches is not so easy, especially since my girlfriend didn't want to follow me in my crazy adventure. Our relationship was crashing down at a rapid speed. I contacted an agent and made an appointment to view an apartment. This exact same day, talking with a friend of mine, I found everything that I needed to secure the apartment I'm living in now. Just the day before, I had received mail from someone who absolutely wanted to attend my seminar about toxic relationships. She was traveling a lot and wanted to know my schedule so she could arrange to come to Paris because she was living in... Nice!

That request was the first of new opportunities which quickly allowed me to work in my new town. I began organizing more and more workshops about yoga and meditation for children and high-potential people. My goal was to help them to live better in their family life and at work. I met wonderful people and soon I had many great opportunities to give workshops all over the world.

I love to talk with people about the flow of life, neuroscience, quantum physics, and I love spending time at the seaside, too. I love traveling, speaking different languages, exploring other cultures and ways of life. Now my clients pay me to do just that.

Miracles now seem to occur in the ways I always wanted them to. Since I got into the habit of listening to my intuition, my gut, and voices from my heart, things are going so much easier. Maybe this is what having faith is? Certainly, this is what being myself, my authentic self feels like.

Now I know that playing it safe actually put my true self in danger. I know that social success does not have to cost me my health and wellbeing—it is the result of self-consciousness and self-esteem.

I keep on attending seminars and workshops, but not for the same reasons. I don't want to succeed in life; I want to fully live my life and discover more and more about my authentic self. Whatever it is, I know I must love myself as I am and then I will become as I'd like.

Now I know that I was wrong to wait for wealth to feel abundant and worthy. I was wrong to wait for success to feel empowerment. I was wrong to wait to heal to feel gratitude and wholeness. I was wrong to wait for a new relationship to feel love. I was wrong to wait for a mystical experience to feel ecstasy.

Now I know I was a victim of my environment. I was waiting for something outside of myself to change what I felt on the inside. Now I know I was empty. I was in lack, suffering and waiting for some external conditions to change how I was feeling. And when it didn't happen how I wanted, I was losing my energy to fight it, trying to control and manipulate it, trying to make it happen because I was separate from my authentic self and its infinite possibilities.

Now I know that the moment I start to feel wholeness, my healing begins. The moment I start to feel worthy, I begin to reach my goals. The moment I feel empowered, synchronicity begins to happen all around me. The moment I decide to rhapsodize, I begin to live a mystical experience. The moment I'm in love with myself and in love with life, I magnetize an equal partner.

And that what's happened. By the merest chance, while I was in a place where I should not be, at the time I had not planned to be there, I met Eve—the first woman to love me in such a way that makes me feel free. This kind of relationship is so fresh that I still feel like a newcomer, a novice in real love. My time to rise called for me and I woke up. My time to rise is now and waking up is living in the present moment.

Since I arrived in Nice, every single day, I write thirty times on a white sheet of paper with a blue pen "I love myself, I approve myself, I prefer myself, and I congratulate myself." I have filled many notebooks with these powerful words. I meditate every single day on how to apply it to all situations of everyday life. I'm convinced that what's happening now is the direct result of that simple exercise. All the people I coach think so, too.

About the Author

Romeo Cournal is an Intuitive Life Coach. He shares his expertise about toxic relationships and gifted people for francophones. It is said that he has never been wrong in his job. He invites and accompanies all those who want to find their own path to self. His motto is: "I love myself, I approve myself, I prefer myself, and I congratulate myself." If you want to learn how to be proudly peaceful and truly happy every day, this passionate education in neuroscience and quantum physics is waiting for you at: www.romeocournal.com

Armor and Stilettos

Geneviève Pépin

Head First

I know I am meant for great things. I am going to be up there with the greatest, making tons of money, and drinking expensive cocktails in fancy bars. I see myself walking through a buzzing cosmopolitan city, in my well-fitted suit and stilettos, with the wind in my hair. Yes sir, I am going to play big! But in the meantime, I need to work my ass off. So here I am, walking through the empty university corridor at 7:00 AM, at a brisk pace, my head high. The brand new day ahead of me is a new beginning, a clean slate to accomplish more. Armed with my to-do list and a willingness to do whatever it takes, I am determined to be my most professional and organized, so the path will lead me to guaranteed success.

Oh damn it! My optimistic chain of thought is interrupted as I see a fellow student walking toward me. I feel a pressure in my chest, my throat tightens and look down. *Say something, or you'll look stupid.* I raise my head, put a smile on my face, turn on my perky attitude and say "Good morning! You're here so early! I'll see you in the meeting." We are both part of a handpicked team of international trade delegates, the first cohort to go to China in the name of the university, to represent local businesses. Let's just say there is a lot of expectations on that team, and at least, a lot of pride to be on it. Why am I so nervous about running into a teammate? Because I still don't know what the heck I am doing on that team. Everyone on it has more experience, a better background, or higher grades than I have. I really don't even fully understand what I am going to do , but I know it's going to look great on my resume. *You fooled them enough to get in. Don't blow it now.*

Finding Comfort in Discomfort

– One year later –

Not only did I not blow it and succeed as a trade delegate, the project helped me get a full scholarship to China for a year. Talk about a shiny experience to display on my CV! The only downside is they wouldn't let me study business here. The scholarship committee gave priority to students with an interest in studying the Chinese language. That was not my case at all, but after being rejected for business, I did the application as a language student *et voilà*! I am now battling with those little characters for a year. Life is good here. China is just so different, and every day is an adventure. It challenges every aspect of what I know, from my daily interactions, to what I perceive as possible. The more I decipher the language, the more I am hooked. I even get a buzz from having a simple conversation with the Chinese man fixing bikes on the side of the street. Talk about something I never thought I would do.

To my own surprise, I find myself filling an application to renew my scholarship and get on board for a second year, delaying my business studies. *Learning Chinese in this era is a no-brainer hello endless job opportunities!* Although at this point, I have no idea what job opportunities I am talking about. But I'm enjoying this experience too much to worry about it—THIS, is just the beginning.

Rising Expectations

– Two years later –

As I walk in a circle, I'm pulling my hair out, wondering, *What if nobody comes? What if the event is a flop?* My breath is short, my throat is tight, my thoughts are jumping around like lottery balls in their spinning machine. *I should have known I couldn't do this.* I foolishly took on the organization of the first business event of my student association. Of course, I have no idea what I am doing. I already picture the disappointed look on my superior's face when I don't fulfill their expectations. I imagine my colleagues patting me on the back while thinking I don't have what it takes. I see myself losing the 'Achiever' badge of honour I was wearing so proudly. .

This is the first time I experience that level of anxiety – I feel like my head won't let me rest. I am back from China, once again into my business studies, and at my parents' hourse. I am doing every school association and project I could possibly sign up for. You know, it looks good on a resume. I am now trilingual, I speak French, Chinese and English. I have built skills and experiences that are highly regarded, and I feel I need to live up to everyone's expectation. *"You are a machine!"* they say. *If it doesn't work out, what am I good for?* Why would I do all of that work, get all of that experience, spend all that money, if not to thrive when I am back home? *Don't blow this!*

A week later, I stumble out of the doctor's office with a diagnosis of depression.

The Perfect Fit...Or Not Quite

– One year later–

Back on Chinese land, I just landed a short contract at the Consulate and I am already in touch with leaders of the incoming Premier mission. My mom is proud. For me, it's the perfect balance between work security and exciting opportunities.

As I walk into the hotel meeting room and find my seat in front of the Premier's Chief of Cabinet, I feel fine. I smell the luxury hotel's fresh signature fragrance. The carpet is so thick under my stiletto heels that I have a hard time not stumbling as I try to walk confidently to my seat, with the little range of motion that my pencil skirt allows. I sit up straight while organizing my notes. I know the logistics of the event by heart. I have been briefed on how to act if I don't know the answer. I know what I need to know. And I look *awesome* in my suit. All good to go!

As we are having a conversation about the details of the event, I feel empowered until I am told to stop asking questions and only speak when I am told to.

Bubble popped.

I know he is not coming from a bad place. That's how it is here, nothing personal. As I sense my face turning red, I have another realization. It's like a bright light illuminating a dark room. I want to be in a position where I am rewarded for my initiative and creativity; for the go-getter that I am. Not for answering questions or only speaking when directed. I sneak a peak at the other coordinators—who showed up to the meeting exhausted and on the edge of burnout—sipping their fourth watery coffee.

This is not for me. Sorry, mom, change of plans.

I want to create positive change. I'm gonna change lives y'all!

On The Right Foot

– Three months later –

I wake up on a friend's couch, and I feel the nervous energies of butterflies fluttering in my stomach. I stand up, ecstatic. I got my answer from the interview—I was hired as a project manager to start the Chinese branch of a company I love because it has a social purpose. I text one of my closest friends: *I made it! Starting today, I will get up every morning to make a positive change in the world.* Now, this all makes sense. I am on the right track. This is the challenge I have been waiting for and I am more determined than ever to make it. I know it's going to be hard, but this is the perfect job for me. Like

Frank Sinatra sang: "If I can make it there, I can make it anywhere." Bring it on!

Lost and Numb

– One year later –

I skillfully steal some chopsticks on my way to the restaurant bathroom and hide them in my sleeve. I bend over the squat toilet, put the chopsticks down my throat and make the food come back up. I sigh deeply. This is my coping mechanism, like I am stripping away my shame. It's a short moment of escape, when my thoughts go silent, when the pressure goes away. I get better at it every time. I know what to use, when to do it, how to cover it. No problem. It's only temporary anyway. I'll be doing better soon. I'm just going through a rough patch at work, just growing pains. *If I work harder I'll get through it. If I eat less I'll get through it. If I am more disciplined I'll get through it.* The important part for now, is to look like I know what I am doing.

Cracked Open

– Two years later –

I am on a stage in front of 400 business people, diplomats, ministers, board members, and the Premier. This event is one of the biggest and most important I have ever put together, as the head of my department at a national business organization.

I host in three languages in front of the crowd. People congratulate me, thank me for my work. I get praises from the cabinet, the same one I was sitting in front of three years earlier. I take a picture with the Premier and send it to my mom. I know she will be proud, and finally see that all I've been through now makes sense. I won't lie, I am exhausted, but in this moment, I feel like a star.

A week later, I am on my scooter, riding across Shanghai, with a McDonald's meal on my back seat. I park and climb the stairs to my tiny apartment. This feels weird. It's like somebody else is in my body. I have a hard time controlling my movements. The apartment is silent and I feel empty inside. I hear the rustle of the brown paper bag as I grab more fries. I have no intention of keeping the food in. I need to get it out. It's painful but it makes me feel in control. A few minutes later, I feel dizzy and warm, finding comfort in the cold ceramic bathroom floor.

As I walk back from the bathroom, I see someone in the mirror. She has a red, puffy face and her swollen bloodshot eyes are filled with tears. *Who's that girl? Is that me?* I can't ignore the truth anymore, it is staring right at me…*but…I thought…I was happy.*

I don't recognize myself. *Why am I doing this? WHO am I doing this for?*

For a split second of clarity, I see the bigger picture. Me, alone in my Shanghai apartment, crying on a Saturday afternoon. My family and my boyfriend are far away on two different continents. My desired path not getting any closer. Is *this* what I signed up for? Nothing makes sense anymore.

Within 24 hours, I have a one way ticket booked for Spain to join the love of my life, as I leave everything behind.

Everything But Me

– Two years later –

Sitting at my desk, I am battling my eyes strain from the irritating combination of yellow lighting in my office and my computer screen. Now living in Spain, I am happily married and with a well paid managerial job in a multinational company, where I can use my creativity in my marketing role. I am on my way to getting my coaching certification on the side, and will use those skills at work. My husband and I have a kick-ass apartment in the center of the city, and I find great joy in rocking my perfectly assembled work outfits. I healed my eating disorder, and am getting help from a coach to continue improving myself. My life is rebuilt. I feel very lucky.

Walking home straight out of a meeting with the CEO, I feel my throat closing up. I'm having a hard time breathing. I am walking faster and faster to get home, stumbling on the uneven cobblestone road. It is my first anxiety attack in a long time. Once I get home all I can think about is how angry I am with myself. I have everything I asked for and yet here I am, once again crying on the couch.... *What's the matter with you girl? Seriously?*

In between gasps of air, it becomes clear. There is one common denominator in all of those experiences: me. That inner battle between the "right" and the "real" is no longer bearable. I can no longer let that desire for approval keep guiding my decisions. I have risked everything to be who I think I should be, including my life. Now, I only see one choice left—risking my pride.

Untying My Chains

– Six months later –

It takes all I have to loosen the grip on my idea of success. This idea of that determined, successful professional who can bear it all with her stilettos and steel-plated armor, has failed. After all, my armor is not that thick, and it crumbles a little more with each hit. Most of which, come from me.

With the help of my coach, and with the unconditional support of my husband, I finally decide to take off my mask, and give myself permission.

Permission to start again.

Permission to want what I want.

Permission to be who I am, who *I* want to be.

Permission to take up space.

Permission to receive.

Recognizing what I can and can't control, I learn to know myself, and to love myself *first*. Only in that way can I be of true service to others.

I quit my job.

I start a fashion project. I sing in public. I become a coach.

I take sporadic jobs, I invest time and money.

I run out of money and recalculate.

I fail.

I learn.

I get up.

I start from scratch.

I keep going…

I learn how to forgive myself.

For not being perfect.

For falling down.

For following the process and learning along the way.

For being great at some things, and so-so at others.

I recognize and accept fear.

The fear that is uncomfortable.

The fear that makes my whole body numb, like I am high.

I accept it, I thank it, and I move beyond it.

Don't get me wrong, I will fall again, I will be criticized again. And I will get up again. I know none of it defines who I am. I am still hungry and ambitious—I am rising.

I hope my story will inspire you to find the power you have within and to give yourself the permission you need. Sometimes the self is buried so deep down that we forget it's even there. But with time, it screams so loudly it becomes impossible to ignore. Feeling good about who you are at every stage is the greatest gift you can give yourself.

If that resonates with you, feel free to drop me a line at hello@nettolacoaching.com

It is never too late to be who you want to be.

About the Author

Geneviève Pépin is an accredited life coach on a mission to help women around the world feel great about themselves from the inside out. She provides actionable coaching to help her clients realign their life with who they really are, let go of what is holding them back and take their journey on a whole other level. Join her at

www.nettolacoaching.com, or say hello at hello@nettolacoaching.com to schedule a free consultation.

TIME TO RISE

4

MY LIFE, MY WAY

Dying to Live My Life

Janet L. Anthony, PhD

I am so tired of listening to everyone else's joy and happiness. I want to share my happiness, but the problem is it doesn't feel like happiness to me. My friends share so much of their special moments with me that I feel envious at times. Instead of sharing my joy and successes, it seems like the only thing I can share are life's bitter moments of struggles, disappointments, and frustration. I feel trapped by the cares of my world—like I'm a bother to others. I just can't live like this anymore. It's like every ounce of hope I had has been choked out of my very soul. Living like this is absolutely too much! Maybe the best way to deal with this unhappiness is to go to sleep forever. Then I won't feel like I'm a bother to anyone else. If only my divine Creator would grant me this one request and allow me to peacefully sleep in His arms, my life and others would be so much better.

Obviously my request to sleep eternally went unfulfilled. I'm still here, eight months later. Why do I think I am still here? Well, let's just say a series of questions and visions interrupted the course of my quest.

Lies I Believed

Replaying that scenario in my mind has me choked to tears. I never imagined coming to terms with being depressed. Not even a doctor could tell me I was depressed prior to me accepting it. Depression was not an option. I'm a doctoral recipient for goodness sake! C'mon? *Depressed?* Nah, not me, I'm not depressed. I'm academically accomplished, I have my own house, cars, a dog, I mean how can anyone think I'm depressed? Yet, every morning before my feet even hit the floor, I was greeted by a hearty heaviness and a cloud of misery sent to remind me how worthless I am. By the time I did get out of the bed, I could barely look at

196

myself in the mirror because I already believed, *something is wrong with me.* This one thought, or should I say "lie," set the course of my day every day. And, God forbid something transpired throughout the course of the day suggesting I didn't do something right…oh my goodness, the whole day was shot. Immediately, I was plagued by multiple lies: "God doesn't love me like He loves others," "I can't make anyone happy." "I'll never be good enough." "Maybe this is all God wants me to have." Every lie that was said and each lie I believed led me to accept I am a bother to others and I am not worthy to be here. So, it seemed to me the best solution would be to permanently go to sleep.

The Awakening

Yet, before I could even close my eyes to go to sleep, I heard in my mind, *You mean go to sleep to your fleshly desires? You mean go to sleep to men pleasing? Do you mean go to sleep to what others have said about you? These things I have expected of you to go to sleep to.* The rapid-fire questions stumped me so that all I could say was, "Yes, I guess so." When I said yes, a fresh wind entered my body.

This wind breathed life into me and showed me the most beautiful woman I'd ever seen. As I looked closer at her, I noticed that the woman was me; the *real* me. A fulfilled part of me living and loving the best version of me. Instead of embracing the melancholic tune, "What's wrong with me? This part of me created a melody. It was a melody that vibrated the very fibers of my being and harmoniously bellowed, "I LOVE ME!" This was the most beautiful sound to hear and vision to see. Everything I envied of others, this woman possessed and so much more. She was vibrant, empowered, and inspired to live. The image of fulfillment, wholeness, and contentment stood confidently before me. Then in a blink of an eye, the vision was gone.

It felt like that breath of life was snatched right out of me. The heaviness I felt before returned, but this time turmoil and chaos returned with it. These two critics stirred inner conflict between who I saw and who I was, causing me to ask myself, "What happened? One minute the best part of me was here and now she's gone? Why? I want her back! Why did this breathtaking beauty go away?"

I was totally confused. I felt stuck between the vision and my reality. Nevertheless, that moment awakened me to something greater, and I wanted it. Neither confusion nor depression was going to stop me from meeting and becoming her. For once, I was determined to capture the beauty of her no matter what. And, from that day forward, I purposed in my heart to walk in this new identity. But, attaining this beauty came with a cost.

Cost 1: Recognize the Chameleon Behavior

Have you ever been in a situation where you wanted to mesh and mold with others so badly you'd compromise the unknown part of you to become known? You want to be you, but because you have never been you, you decided to present the most comfortable version of you? This, my friend, I call it chameleonizing. Instead of being the most beautiful, original version of you, you opt to present your own perceptional reality to "fit in." This behavior can be overwhelming and even downright frustrating. As a chameleon, you sometimes exaggerate your character. Depending on the setting, chameleon-like behavior will often exaggerate humor just to be accepted, or it may have you spiraling downward into feeling rejected. The nature of the chameleon goes into protection mode, which releases a negative energy from the lies you already believed about yourself. But, the number one reason this chameleon-like behavior manifests is because you have yet to meet, accept, and embrace the real you.

This was my problem for a long time. I didn't know me. I wasn't comfortable living the life of the woman I saw in the vision. And, I didn't know how to be the woman in the vision without being judged as "someone I'm not."

The art of chameleonizing was natural for me. The lies either sheltered me from fear of rejection or abandonment, or protected me from being hurt or disappointed. Yet, little did friends, family, associates, and coworkers know, this was the *illusion* of me not the *real* me. The more I chameleonized the more I suppressed the authentic me. Being the chameleon seemed easier to me. The only problem with this form of mimicry was I held the liberated, authentic me hostage to my fear of change.

Cost 2: Deconstruct the Chameleon Identity

I was comfortable living the chameleon lifestyle; it made me who I was. However, I was miserable living this reality. I had to change the way I saw myself, but I didn't know where or how to begin.

I hired a coach to help me deconstruct this chameleon identity. After our first conversation, I immediately knew chameleonizing was not going to help me meet the real me. When you chameleonize, you can fool everyone around you, but when the right person is assigned to help you evolve into your true identity, chameleonizing is not an option. You must be open, present, and willing to be transparent.

The coach suggested journaling, which turned out to be critical to discovering the real me. I found this process relaxing because it was the only place I could be me without feeling judged by others. I could be vulnerable and honest with myself. I could locate the critic within and challenge assumptions that affected the way I perceived myself. There were moments when the journaling process was brutal and upsetting, yet it gave me clarity and insight.

For example, one of the journal assignments given by my coach was to accept that I do matter and I am valuable. Yet, the conflict between what he said and what I believed led me to ask, "If I matter, why do I feel like I don't?" While pondering this question and searching for answers, I finally heard a still, small voice say,

"You do matter and this season of torment and questioning is over! I don't want you to conform anymore to please someone or be someone you are not. You are so much more than a chameleon. I never created you to hide or mimic anyone else. You chameleonized because you were afraid. Afraid to be who I called and made you to be. Yes, life, people, circumstances kicked you in the gut, and I AM was and will be there to help you. Disappointment and heartbreak attempted to rip you apart, and I AM was and will be there to mend the broken pieces. No longer will you chameleonize that's not why I created you. All I want is for you to be who I created you to be. When you feel lonely, dismayed, or unimportant, know I AM will always be there."

~ (Psalm 34:18-22 Message Bible).

I captured this moment in writing with tears of joy streaming down my face. The woman I saw before was now moving and breathing within me. I truly felt alive. The lies that sheltered and protected me were shattered. I was finally free to be me, and encouraged to pursue and know more about the core beauty of me.

Cost 3: Find Your Power Five

I was closer now than ever before to fully embracing the woman envisioned. The problem was I still needed to get to know her. Learning about this new me was completely different from the chameleon I used to be. But, how was I supposed to get acquainted with her? The discovery of this answer began with a reality check from my mentor saying, "The only way you are going to ever manifest your epic being is taking time away from others to learn, love, and appreciate you." This statement could not be further from the truth.

It was time for me to live "in" purpose intentionally. To do that meant *detaching* from those who were familiar with me and *connecting* with those who would help me become the best part of me. Therefore, I connected with five people who were accomplished and lived what I wanted to see in my life; they each lived a happy and fulfilling life; and each one was not afraid to speak the truth and hold me accountable to my commitment for personal change. They were my Power Five.

Cost 4: Drop the Worthless Mentality

Although my Power Five were from various parts of the world, each one had the same message to me: Accept your value, worth, and inner beauty. For a month straight, each one, at different times, constantly reminded me that I am "fearfully and wonderfully made." I wanted to believe their affirmation, but I struggled with accepting it as a form of confirmation. Although I knew I no longer had to chameleonize, I struggled with embracing what they could see in me. I knew I was free to be me, but I wasn't comfortable with accepting and loving me.

One morning I decided to stay in bed longer than usual. While quietly lying there, I heard that same still, small voice from before now asking me, "What does fearfully mean?" I responded, "One who is full of fear." I waited patiently for more insight to the question. When no other question or answer came to mind, I took it upon myself to search for the meaning of fearfully. To my surprise, I discovered fearfully meant so much more than full of fear. According to the Hebrew concordance, fearfully actually means with great reverence, and a heartfelt interest with respect.

Wow! *Fearfully* and *wonderfully made* finally made sense to me. I now understood fearfully to mean I was intentionally created, shaped, and molded for and with a purpose. A purpose that only I can do and not anyone else. My divine Creator took such a personal interest in me that even His thumbprint and DNA are placed upon and within me. I knew then I was not a mistake.

Cost 5: Love and Accept All of Me

I was so overjoyed to learn I was intentionally created. This made my life totally complete. However, my Creator knew I needed more to sustain me, and that something more was love. I thought at this point I did love me, but I soon learned I was in love with the idea of being me. So, the still, small voice came once again and said:

"Janet, I want you to know I love you. I love you for who you are, I love you for what you do, I love you for all that you bring to the table. You do not have to be afraid. I won't let anyone hurt you. I love you with my whole heart and you are safe with me. You are loved and protected by my love. I love you for you and you are okay. I love you my princess, my baby girl. Always remember, God the Father, has you in the palm of His hands. He intentionally shaped, molded, created you to be in His very image. So, love and accept all of you. You are not a mistake, don't lose yourself to someone else's idea of you, and hold on to your value because you are loved."

Now, I get it and I feel absolutely complete! After capturing this love epiphany in writing, I finally believe and I feel whole, and I feel love, and fulfillment. I am no longer torn between the vision and reality, and I no longer battle between two identities. I finally live the liberated me I saw in the vision.

Although it took a long time to get here, I made it! I am finally here! And I am not here without a price. As you have read, each stage cost me something, but it was well worth the investment. This transformation was not easy as each stage caused pain and heartache, but the reward at the end was well worth it. Nothing compares to knowing who I am. And nothing will compare to knowing who you are. I urge you today, to go through the discovery process of learning and knowing more about you—the authentic you. So you too will be like me, able to boldly, confidently and joyfully declare, "I love the fearfully, wonderfully, uniquely made imperfect me!"

About the Author

Dr. Janet L. Anthony is a respected Associate Professor of Literacy at Mott Community College in Flint, MI. She is the author of *Strategic Reading Skills for the College Students: A Guide to Student Success.* She founded and writes for Personal Touch Consulting Services, LLC. Her personal awakening has motivated her to walk in liberty and unashamedly share her victory over depression into oneness. She is moved by inspiration and loves to candidly share her life experiences to help you live your best and most fulfilling life now! To reach Dr. Anthony contact: tenaj_ptc@yahoo.com or call (810) 221-5873.

Rise & Shine

Todd Malloy

I was born to do this and I won't apologize for being me!

Today I stand, 6'4", 240 pounds with an athletic build. Some might even say I am tall, dark, and handsome. (I smile as I write this.) I have advanced degrees and professional certifications. I am a therapist, an academic lecturer, a public speaker, and a show developer and producer.

When I was a child, some people called me skinny, dark, nappy-headed, and a few even said that I wouldn't amount to much. I grew up in the 1960's in New England in a low-income housing project with a single-parent mother and my younger brother, so it's no real surprise that people thought that. We were the picture of every negative race, class, and gender stereotype. Add to that a dad who abandoned us when I was five years old, who I later learned left because he did not see spending the rest of his life "with hillbillies."

During that period, unknown to me, a tapestry was being created to shape and mold me into the person societal predators interpreted (and probably wanted) me to be—without any consideration or input from me. And it would be years before I realized how to live an authentic, true self life...a life of being present, engaged, empowered, and joyful. I reached this point by using the keys of freedom that I outline below.

Listen to Your Soul

There was confusion, wonder, and bewilderment to me, about what it meant for a marginalized five-year-old boy to be the "man of the house." These complexity of feelings killed off many emotional connections and birthed a mindset of, "life has nothing to do with likes or dislikes, just shit that has to be dealt with."

Between consoling an emotionally distraught and overwhelmed mother, navigating solicitations to be in gangs and to run numbers, managing the peer pressure to be like everybody else, and facing a constant lack of support and resources, a key was given to me. The same mother who was desperate to be told that everything would be all right, also taught her boys that their lives were not limited or defined by the six blocks that surrounded them. She took my brother and me to the amusement park at Coney Island in New York. We took a train ride, stayed in a hotel, ordered room service, and ran smiling and laughing through the adjoining rooms. We had so much fun. It was a time when we were happy, and it was evidence that life could be joyful. I truly believe it was in that moment, that the will to personally grow and develop was sparked in me. I experienced excitement, joy, and a sense of freedom that stayed deep within me over the years.

When I turned seventeen, I was at a pivotal crossroad in my life. As part of my final year in high school, seniors spent a day in a work environment that corresponded to his or her interests and career goals. Mine was psychiatry, so I was given the opportunity to spend the day at a local medical school. It was a sunny, mild day in May of 1980, and I felt free, I also felt something that I don't think I'd ever felt before. After arriving, I sat in the meeting room as the doctors and interns introduced themselves and explained the flow of the day. I had found a seat up front and was all smiles, although I was the only person in the room who looked like me. Sitting in front is one of the quirks I have still have. It started out as a response to racial injustices, and these days, being hearing impaired, it helps me to hear better.

My soul moved through the day from a place of knowing that I belong. My truth, that I was in the right place, pursuing the right goal was being recognized and acknowledged in every experience of the day. It was in my posture, my openness to others, and a willingness to engage in conversation. I had made it through the muck and mire of life to a point where everything was starting to make sense. I understood the value of aligning with my authentic self and not the stereotype. I was experiencing the wonders of medical science and the human body. I had touched cadavers, seen human guts and organs, and walked through the wondrous labs filled with amazing equipment. This day I strode ahead of my classmates, as I listened to the intern in the long white coat who led the day.

Then the moment of truth. The intern turned around, looked at me and said, "What do you want to be?" The biggest smiled spread across my face, you know the one where you show all thirty-two teeth, and I said excitedly, "I want to be a psychiatrist!" He smiled and replied, "You have twelve more years of school!" My joy died instantly. I was flooded with an overwhelming sense of defeat. From my perspective, I had worked so hard to get to that point. I would be the first member of my family to graduate from high school. I helped to pay for my own catholic school education by working as a dishwasher in a hospital kitchen. My mother could not afford for me to go to college for four years, let alone *twelve* years.

At this crossroad, I reacted as many people do. I focused on all the reasons it *couldn't* happen. I consciously let go of my truth and chose safety. I changed my pursuit from what I believe I was *born* to do, to identifying, academically, what I was *good* at—math and science—and chose to be an engineer. And, the winding, twisting, curving, bumpy, road to my authentic self began.

Never Give Up on Your Dreams

Ten years later, through much trial and tribulation, I became an engineer, a respectable profession that seemed impressive to others. But it was not my truth. After my college graduation ceremony, with the cheers of my family for my accomplishment still ringing in my ears, I went into my room and burst into tears. I cried because I knew I would become successful at something I did not want to do. Little did I know this testimony would have value, because in time I would reclaim the path to my purpose.

Throughout the journey of twists and turns to reach this point, there was an inner force that continued to pull me to my joyful memory of how I felt that special day when I was seventeen and had found my truth. Though the trials and tribulation of life seemed to hold me back, I learned the keys that propelled me toward that freeing feeling, toward my truth. I became aware of the benefits of perseverance, discipline, strength, and of forgiving myself for a multitude of errors and ridiculous risks that I'd taken. I learned when all hell breaks loose, not to allow my emotions to control me, but to instead, control my emotions. My mother taught me that lesson when I was a child. She said, "the one who controls your emotions controls you."

Capitalize on the Depths of Your Experiences, Frailties, and Challenges

Armed with skills that fostered my growth and development, yet struggling internally with the choice that I made at seventeen years old, I continued to live life in the safe lane. As I progressed in my career, I experienced emotions of deep contempt and complacency. Recalling the popular Dunkin' Donuts commercial of the 1980's, the baker got up every morning and said, "It's time to make the donuts." I repeated that statement daily when I got up for work. I was working for a Fortune 500 technology company, and I couldn't imagine one more day of the same routine, mundane work. I was responsible for mechanical design, project scope, test development, production process and prototype build. None of which spoke to my truth and because of it I often felt fed up. Life seemed dull and colorless, like I was going through the motions.

One day, while staring blankly at my computer screen my inner voice said, "I can't do this anymore." In that instant I knew it was time to chart my course for a way out of the safe lane as an engineer and into my rightful place as a therapist. That's when my journey to my authentic self-picked up momentum. Although this marked a time of clarity, it was also a time of fear, wonder, and doubt. I'd become comfortable with the systems I had built in the safe lane and I questioned myself. What about the time and money I had invested in my work? What about my quality of life? What if I failed? What would my family and friends think? But the feeling of wanting and desiring more than my life as an engineer would not go away.

I found the courage to pursue the life that I desired. I shared my new truth with only my closest friends...for *accountability*, not for *permission*. I quickly came to understand that the journey would require faith, courage, wisdom, and strategy. For each step I took in faith, a plank of support was placed under my feet to support me and get me to the next step. I kept my mind open to new possibilities and steadied myself for any challenges on my path.

Get Comfortable With the Uncomfortable

Through life, I have come to understand that the only person who can limit me, is *me*. I would not be limited to be a dude on the block, a gang banger, drug dealer, numbers runner, hustler or the like. These were all examples of a stereotypical life tapestry that was formed based on my circumstances in life. Instead of letting go of my dream to be a psychiatrist, I could have asked myself the question, "How can I do it?" People have always done the "impossible." We've sailed across the globe, broken the sound barrier, sent rockets to the moon, created the World Wide Web, and digital film and audio. Whether I was conscious of this or not, throughout my life experiences an old life tapestry was being unraveled and a new life tapestry, one that would propel me to my true path, was being created. And, there were lessons to be learned through my emotional experiences.

I have learned that to be successful in living life to the fullest, we must come to understand that a variety of emotions are to be expected. Life is laced with threads of joy, sadness, happiness, victimization, excitement, pain, wonder, shame, pleasure, hurt, pride and fear. These emotions are a part of the natural order of life. I have come to realize that our emotions are here to guide us through life. Fear should not cause you to become stuck or make rash decisions. It is a warning to inform you to slow down, to be cautious, and to be strategic about your next move. Our emotions tell us that we should be present, honest, and sincere in every moment. They are not meant to cause us to become stuck, resentful or bitter, but rather to cultivate character, the strength of determination, and our will to thrive. In the process of unravelling an old life tapestry of negative experiences and setbacks to build a new life tapestry of joy and freedom, we must be willing to be comfortable in the uncomfortable. Once we learn how to do this, I believe, nothing can stop us.

Challenge Yourself to Function as Your Greatest Self

Reflecting on this part of my journey, to be my greatest self, I am reminded of how the old life tapestry was woven so tightly that I felt caught within its fray. I was bound so tightly in the threads, that I didn't know where it ended and I began.

I've wondered at times, if when people see me today, the "me" that has inspired and helped so many others to achieve their career goals or personal and emotional wellness, do they realize how far I've come? That at five years old, my skinny, "nappy-headed" self-became the "man of the house." Reflecting on the past, a period that didn't include me or my voice as a significant factor, I now realize that it was not all bad and that the past torment and at times, seemingly overwhelming responsibilities built character and value. Over time it revealed itself as a pathway to wisdom, strength, determination, and the joy and power within my true self.

Be Present, Honest, and Sincere in Every Moment

I know now that there is no such thing as failure. It is a falsehood; there are only lessons to be learned that come from the many layers and dimensions of life. Nothing is designed to destroy us, but rather life is designed to build, shape, mold, and prepare us for purpose and destiny… should we choose to allow it. There were no external forces, being, or energy, that was ever a hindrance in my life. It was my reaction to life, to the choices and decisions I made that fostered either turbulent twists and turns, or great joy and success.

I find this understanding to be empowering because it opens the door to my awareness of how *powerful* I am. In the poem "Invictus" by William Ernest Henley he writes, "I am the master of my fate, I am the captain of my soul." I get it, now.

Between the twist and turns through life, of the five-year-old boy to the man I am today, there was an abundance of what appeared to be delays, false starts, detours, and devastations. That in-between journey, took me through a Fortune 500 corporate career in technology, manufacturing, project management, marketing, sales, ministry, community service, and a few others. There have been great joy, a wealth of knowledge, and the character to redesign the old life tapestry so that I can realize and revision the new life tapestry of my truth.

When I reflect on times of my indirect and eclectic path, filled with the twist and turns of my errors, flaws, and ridiculous risks, I wonder if they were ever *real* mistakes. Or was it instead, the perfect collection of experiences, designed by a greater force, to equip me for the joy that is rightfully mine, because it ultimately allowed me to be me. However, I got here, I am born to do this and won't apologize for it!

I challenge you to look at your tapestries and find the keys to your authentic self…and to be present honest and sincere in every moment.

About the Author

Todd Malloy is a relationship and sex therapist in private practice in Charlotte, NC, USA. He is an academic lecturer, a public speaker, and a show developer and producer. For more information on enabling your inner power to celebrate and live an empowered life, visit www.innerpeacecounselingcenter.com, mancave conversations.com, or call (704) 937-2286.

From Strong to Awesome

Leslie van Oostenbrugge

There I was, picking up the pieces…

Literally, because I had smashed an expensive designer chair against the wall in my new office. Figuratively, because I was desperately trying to repair my emotional and financial situation.

How was I going to get out of this predicament, which I blamed my former colleague for? I had decided to leave our partnership to finally start my own dental practice. My heart had already told me to do so many years prior. My mind however demanded I stay because of "what would they think of me-it is." You know, the sickness people have when they sacrifice their life and happiness to conform. But this was the last straw. Without consulting me, my colleague had decided to make a financial decision and I *literally* had to pay for it. That moment left me in total shock and devastation. That was when I decided it was time to go. <u>How much more did I have to take?</u>

Early the next morning I called a contractor with whom I had worked before to make to discuss with him the specifics of my own dental office. His first words to me were: "I was expecting your call." That took me by surprise. I'd made the decision yesterday, how could he be expecting my call? But I'm getting ahead of myself. Before I could open my own office I first had to talk with the bank to secure a loan. A few months later they gave me the green light for a mortgage, and off I went with my contractor to look for a new location.

All Things Work Together For Good

Two years later, in 2009, I was settled in a brilliant new space. Although I still felt guilty leaving my colleague behind I knew I had made one of the best decisions in my life. I worked with my team to get the new office organized. Then it all came crashing down. Because of miscalculations about how much money was needed to finish, it became all too clear, that the money I had gotten from the bank was not enough. Unexpected work had to be done and on top of that expense, I was sued by my colleague.

This was why I had smashed the chair. While picking up the pieces of the chair I thought, *there must be a better way!*

I don't often descend into despair. Quite the opposite, I am funny, uplifting, happy, mischievous. What happened to me? Why wasn't I able to get my finances straight? I wasn't used to failure, in fact, I had succeeded in everything I attempted in my life. I finished two professional studies programs, was an excellent dentist (according to my patients), did well in sports, did volunteer work, had a beautiful home, and best of all—I was happy.

Then I heard it. A whisper…a voice telling me to "read."

Read? Read what? I wondered. Where was this voice coming from? Then I remembered, my assistants had given me Rhonda Byrnes' book *The Power,* back in 2006.

I decided then and there to listen to "The Voice."

I had to get out of the dire financial situation I was in, that was for sure. I had asked for help and I received the answer. I got the book off my shelf and I took it with me everywhere I went—the office, hairdresser, beach, on vacation, to bed. Every single page I read felt like a slap in the face!

I have been spiritual all my life and I'd never thought that spirituality and MONEY could go hand in hand. I thought money was bad, and people who had money were greedy and I never envied them. To me, money was evil and the cause of most problems in the world.

Then learned all about the Law of Attraction—that thoughts are a form of energy and we can use them to manifest what we want in our life. A powerful message stuck with me: "That which is like unto itself is drawn."

What an insightful discovery! If this was really true then it meant that everything happening in my life I had attracted. The more I read about it the more it became clear to me that my relationship with money—I had cursed it for many many years—had created a financial void in my life. Basically *I* had kept it away. Growing up, I learned that we have to work hard for money, and that only certain people have enough of it. To me money became something you had to save, to hoard. To me money was evil.

Clearly the Law of Attraction works, whether you believe it or not, it's a Universal Law. It's also important to know that the universe has your back, that there is a Greater Power, one far greater than we are. Because we don't see it doesn't mean that it isn't there. Consider The Law of Gravity. We cannot see, smell, hear, taste, or touch gravity but we know it's there. Think about what happens when you drop something. We can use of the Law of Gravity purposefully or we can fight it. Regardless of what we do, it is still there. The Law of Attraction is the same way. We can use its energy purposefully or we can fight against it.

If you do not consider yourself worthy of it, money will not come to you. When you think you are not worth that expensive outfit or that delicious bread or that wonderful trip you will indeed *not* be worthy to get them. But how does this attraction work? Is it as simple as thinking about something and receiving it?

I was doubtful, and as an academic I wanted proof. I usually want to know what I am doing and why. So I dove into the latest findings of biology, genetics, neuroscience, and psychology of the law of attraction. I learned that geneticists found that limiting beliefs are inherited! And that psychologists support the use of affirmations! They are positive phrases you repeat to yourself that describe what you want. Over time they overwrite any limiting or negative beliefs and replace them with positive ones. At first these words might not feel true to you, but repetition causes them to sink into your subconscious and create a new belief that then radiates out of you and into the universe.

There is a powerful saying: A belief is just a thought you keep thinking. If that is the case, you can change your thoughts to create your reality and to attract what you want in your life. Affirmations are so powerful that they've been proven to help with recovery from trauma, depression, migraines, and can improve our overall physical health. The power of positive thinking even has a lot of support in medical journals.

Ask And it Will be Given to You

Now, this is something my academic mind could grasp. If the effects of positive affirmations have already been proven and millions of people have benefited from it, why not try it? At this point, what did I have to lose? I'm already spiritual, why not practice a Universal law? From that day on I consciously and deliberately repeated my affirmations for months.

Believing is Seeing

At 6 o'clock, every morning when my alarm goes off, I sit up against my pillows, rub the sleep from my eyes and I give thanks to the universe—God, Source, Buddha. Then I recite my affirmations.

Thank you Universe for giving me another blissful day.

Thank you Universe for giving me these beautiful kids.

Thank you Universe for giving me a healthy body.

Thank you Universe for giving me lovely friends.

Thank you Universe for giving me courage to choose.

Thank you Universe for giving me my humor.

Thank you Universe for giving me endless patience.

.... (fill in the blank)..........................

It takes no longer than five minutes but its effects can be life-changing, *literally*!

Give thanks to whomever or whatever YOU want. Remember, these are affirmations so they should be positive. So an affirmation like: Thank you Universe for helping me *not* fight my neighbor might not be as effective as Thank you Universe for giving me *such lovely* neighbors.

Through daily repetition, these positive thoughts will be embedded in your subconscious and then will radiate out into the universe to create a new belief!

And again…believing is seeing.

You might also consider reading a book that speaks to you and inspires you on a spiritual level, like *The Power* inspired me, or read about the Law of Attraction and how everything is "pure" energy, and learn about the process of "like energy attracting like energy." Reading a few pages of uplifting material before getting out of bed is a great way to start of your day and put you in a positive mindset.

For me, my financial situation was my greatest fear. I had to overcome that. I created a specific affirmations to connect to the universe to address it. Ask and it will be delivered.

Writing down your affirmations has an even stronger effect. So every morning I wrote the same sentence over and over:

Thank you for paying all my bills at the end of the year

Thank you for paying all my bills at the end of the year...

Do NOT ask yourself, "how will this be done?" Just have faith. Also be specific; set a timeline in which you want it to happen!

"A belief is a drilled thought"

Remember, you have to think yourself worthy of something to to be able to receive it.

That was another issue for me. I didn't think I was worthy. "Who do you think you are!" was what I often I heard during my childhood and adolescent years. And because of it, I thought I was nothing. I carried this thought with me for decades until I realized how powerful that thought was because it was creating my reality. And because I was creating it I was the only one to change it.

To that end, I started to do mirror work. It is a conscious way to change your thoughts by repeating positive affirmations while looking in that mirror.

For instance:

"I have beautiful eyes."

"I have strong, muscular arms."

"I love my hair."

'......fill in the blank......'

Very important—don't say something if you don't believe it. Say something else. If you do not believe you have beautiful eyes start with another part of your body, and gradually work your way up or down. Within a few weeks of doing mirror work, it literally changed my mind! I now pass mirrors in stores with a huge grin on my face. So, been there, done that. I now consider myself worthy of anything!

The power is within us. But you have to have faith, not only in the process but in yourself. To conceive you must first believe. And you must be OPEN to receive. Many people ask for help but they don't wait for the answer. It took us years to get where we are, getting out of it won't happen overnight. So don't GIVE UP! The universe w a n t s to give what you need. Give it time to respond. On earth we need the concept of *time* to receive the answer. So be patient.

The universe is in all things! We human beings are atoms and molecules, we are energy and contain the same atoms and molecules as the universe? Our heart generates the largest electromagnetic field in the body. The field can be detected and measured several feet away from the body. It possesses a level of intelligence that scientist are only now beginning to understand. The heart plays a greater role in our mental, emotional, and physical processes than we had previously thought. And according to several scientific studies, purposely increasing your heart energy, increases the energy field and can improve our life.

Knowing this is helpful when doing your affirmations or mirror work, or as you go through daily life be sure to intentionally *raise* your own heartbeat! We can create our own positive vibe or energy, by thinking of something wonderful, like being in love, or your wonderful kids. You want to keep the vibe so high that it will match the vibe of the universe. When you "open up" your heart you can create a love filled energy, which is a powerful catalyst.

Remember, negative thoughts create negative energy. You are born whole, opening up to the universe is your birthright. You just lost it somewhere in your timeline. It takes practice of course, nothing worth doing comes easily. But in the end, it can change you life and even heal you, like I healed myself from back pain. We didn't come into the world broken we came here whole. At any time we can change our circumstances if we learn to align with the universe and use its positive and powerful energy to create what we want in our life. I know firsthand that it is possible. It took me only several months to realize my first "money come into my life without working" manifestation. Through self-love and positive affirmations I received an unexpected gift of thousands of dollars and also led to the absolution of a tax payment where I owed thousands of dollars! It has since led me to so much more in my life. My dire financial situation was resolved and my bills were all paid off before the end of the year!

I've learned many valuable lessons in that time, that I want to share with you. There is no good or bad. Every person in life is sent to you for a reason. There is no need to blame anyone for anything. YOU needed the lesson and YOU are the teacher. Know that if you want to change your life, you can, but it is up to you.

We are all in this together.

About the Author

Leslie van Oostenbrugge is a passionate holistic dentist. She graduated dental school and the School for Physical Therapy with honors. Her upcoming book *Drilling Into My Emotions* will change numerous lives by curing many dental problems. She is a joyful, and empowering woman. Leslie has a holistic dental office in Vianen, the Netherlands. She teaches the principles of how the universe always has your back, and quite often, your front too! She is known as "the awakening dentist" and her lectures have changed many people's lives—physically, spiritually, and financially. Leslie combines dentistry and spirituality in a new and authentic way. She cannot emphasize enough how important oral health is to our overall health. "Teeth never lie" is her favorite empowering statement!

Leslie is the proud mom of two daughters and one son. She loves her physical workouts and her two doggies.

Visit her online at www.facebook.com/awakeningdentist/ and www.LeslievanOostenbrugge.com

Let Your Life Shine

Lene Kirk

My passion is to guide highly sensitive people to feel their inner power and use their senses as a strength to live a happy life.

My journey to have the knowledge of highly sensitive people and their challenges and strengths starts with my own adventure through my life as a highly sensitive person.

I have transformed the challenges you typically live with as someone who is highly sensitive to strengths. I have prepared and tested all the tools I share on my courses, lecture, blogs and workshops in personal development, transforming communications, mindful living, silent yin, meditation and the meaning of senses.

This adventure starts in my childhood when I became aware that I was different from others. It has made my life an unusual and exciting adventure with a wide radar that captures life around me.

Powerful intuition.

I was a sensitive person with a strong intuition from an early age. Throughout my adult life, I have transformed my challenges into strengths, and develop a method that gives others the possibility of using their own sensitive senses as a strength to find their inner power.

I am a natural listener with a strong intuition – I can feel, read and hear between lines. I experience the world at a high intensity. This can be very draining, but I have developed tools which can make this a powerful force for transformation and happiness.

It has taken many years to rise, but the time is now.

It all started with...

A beautiful little girl with shiny hair, who looked just like a princess. She was very well behaved and had a lot of friends at school.

To the outside world, she was a quiet girl, but not inside her mind. Inside her body and mind was a lot of energy, feelings, conversations and experiences. She tried to explain to people how she felt and what was going on inside. She wanted to share all her thoughts, but nobody wanted to listen. She was told to keep silent. She didn't know why; she thought that everybody was like her. She lived in a world where nobody really listened to her. The little girl had a deep feeling of not belonging in this world physically; she didn't feel like she belonged anywhere.

As time went by, she developed a sort of natural radar to capture how other people felt. It let her read people easily and fit in with everyone to stay out of trouble.

The black box

For a while, she packed all of her inner life into a black box and shut the lid. She made a decision to be like everybody else. Maybe the adults would listen to her and take care of her if she behaved and looked like all the other children. She told herself that it just how it had to be—that she had to look like other children and do the same things as they did. It was frustrating at first, but it eventually became a habit.

The black box remained closed for many years.

She forgot all about the silence and inner power almost. Every time she had an experience, she kept it quiet and didn't tell anybody she saved it in her black box.

The story about the silent girl—that is me.

The time finally came when it was no longer possible to save more experiences in the black box. It was completely full.

I got a sign almost every day, a feeling that told me, "Hey, Lene, what are you going to do with all your inner power?" I really didn't know what to do.

I had a lot of bad experiences and didn't dare to say anything to friends and family because my emotional wounds from childhood and youth were not yet healed.

I didn't know where to go, but I had to fix it—it had to disappear immediately.

My youth

I tried to fix my inner power with physical training, parties, boyfriends, and, unfortunately, an eating disorder. Maybe I have had that eating disorder all my life without even knowing it. When I first become aware of this, many years later, I was told that I was overweight when I was a child. I wasn't, but I tried to fix it anyway. It was a kind of "to be good enough" solution because I believed my thoughts and feelings "were wrong." So how could I be just as good as other people? *Those little thoughts were still there in the back of my mind.*

A kind of extraordinary life.

The only thing I had in my mind was to be like others. I wanted to have an ordinary life… even though I had another feeling inside of me. I felt then and I still do that my life was kind of extraordinary. That I am in this world to contribute with love and energy to people. I had many contradictory feelings and thoughts.

I wasn't happy. I had no feeling of making a difference in my life. I wasn't living an extraordinary life.

I have been stressed twice in my life.

The first time I was stressed was at a time when people didn't really know or talk about stress or the consequences of it. I was totally consumed by my work, often working six days a week from 8 a.m. until 11 p.m. It was an unhealthy and unsustainable life.

I don't think that my boyfriend noticed that I was so stressed, he only wondered whether I cared about myself and our relationship. For two months, I sat in a chair just looking out to see anything.

I was totally empty.

I was just sitting there for weeks. My body was totally "out of order."

One day, everything changed.

In a way, I think I might have meditated for two months. All day, every day and night while sitting in that chair. But suddenly, I was ready to start a new life—a new beginning. I had a powerful feeling of gratitude inside, and rediscovered that I had a body and feelings. I woke up to the fact that I really had to take care of myself.

This awakened a curiosity and appetite for knowledge. I became interested in personal development, spirituality and started my own meditation practice.

It gave me a sense of inner peace no questions and no answers, only peace.

I became aware of my senses. I became conscious, discovering that nature had been a missing link in my life for many years.

I lost contact with my *self* through too much work and became stressed again

I was tired—physically and mentally—and forgot all my intentions. I hadn't changed my habits and the balance between work and leisure was still not correct. By doing my work with other people, I lost myself. I forgot to listen to my heart and fell into a downward spiral. I was too consumed with my work. The company I worked with didn't really care about their employees, they only cared about the money. I was stressed because there was so much negative energy at my job and I had no time to get this out of my system. I lost my energy for everything, and the sight in my right eye nearly disappeared. I quit my job and never went back.

When people don't listen, or when they are dishonest with themselves, I can feel their energy and their feelings. I become tired and irritable. I knew I had to stop immediately, or I would lose my creative mind

A new adventure

I met the man in my life and he has the same feeling of freedom as I have.

Wow! A kind of innocent love.

We got married and now have two lovely children. And with this, a new adventure through my mind and body began.

Now I had to listen to my wisdom.

Stress has told me…

I have been under pressure for a long time, maybe years, without taking responsibility. I had to find out how to manage my new life.

I figured out that it was important for me to live close to nature. I became conscious of my body, food and training, but without dependence. I now enjoy the training in a healthy way and am grateful for my life. I felt and listened to the effect of my attention on my body, mind and heart. I got the feeling that I was getting stronger, both physically and mentally, by listening to my senses and believing that these senses told me the truth.

Yoga was necessary because my body was hypermobile due to a lack of attention in many years. My body and mind were getting stronger and stronger every day. When I started to practice, I got a lot of new insights. I read many books and participated in many courses, workshops and education for years. It became an eternal search for myself. I gained deep insights into my decisions and my internal and external life. I discovered the meaning of listening to my senses, something I now practice a lot.

I was guided to journey deeper into my mind, body and heart.

Now I am a psychotherapist, coach, Feng Shui consultant, and healer. I work with crystal and diet and nutrition. I am also a mindfulness instructor, stress consultant and teacher of meditation and yoga.

For many years, I had the feeling of missing something.

Some friends told me to stop. They said that I was crazy. My husband said that he thought that I wasted all my money, and for what? Just to look inside myself? And maybe he was right. But for me, it was not an option. I had to follow my way and my heart.

My adventure has led me through many educational experiences, discovering other cultures, both with my family and by myself. I have been traveling in Brazil and Peru working with shamans. I have studied culture and nature in New Zealand many other countries. And I found out that I am at home and feel grounded wherever there is nature nearby.

We have traveled a lot for new experiences, and now my grown-up children have been traveling by themselves. I am so proud of them. They have already found their own way.

I have met people who said to me, "why are you using all your money on traveling instead of buying a new car?" But as I told my children, "You can always buy a pair of new shoes, but your feelings and experiences you will have with you for the rest of your life. All those good memories are a kind of developing."

Nature was and still is very important to me. It is the place "to be" and to be in the present.

My wisdom

I found recovery in the wisdom inside of myself, and nature helped me get my energy back. Every day, I spend hours in nature, just walking and being there. It has been a long and beautiful adventure, and it still is. I have my daily meditation practice and yoga. I decided to take an education as a yoga instructor.

Yin yoga, combined with the attention to my senses, has changed my life. I gained a feeling of gratitude. I felt so strong and experienced a release—it's so magical.

Networking

I find it important to network with people with the same positive mindset as me. I gain more energy from them, and they have a natural trust in me, without needing all the details about the credibility of my work. When they have a natural curiosity, and think in creative possibilities instead of limitations and fears, there is no reason to be defensive. People are curious instead of requiring explanations, which depletes my energy.

I decided to start my own yin yoga classes in addition to teaching mindfulness, meditation, breathing exercises, stress prevention and transforming communications.

In my adventure, I have found out that I am a highly sensitive person with highly developed senses. It is very important for me to be grounded with nature. When I am grounded with nature, I feel that I have an inner power. I have also discovered how to practice and work to find my inner power.

I teach people to identify their strongest senses, find their inner power, and show them how to use their sensitivity as a power.

Wisdom and teaching

I have developed silent yin, mindful living, meditations and breathing exercises where you use your strength and senses. Through these practices, it is possible to incorporate a natural strength and silence. It provides a lot of joy and energy, and you automatically become more empathic and creative when you unfold naturally.

I have developed a special relaxation.

Silent relax is a special relaxation where you have the possibility to work with your consciousness in a deep way by listening to your heart and body. You are training your curiosity and how this effects your silence. Listen to your own silence.

The training uses easy tools in a natural way in your daily life, and you will preserve your life energy.

My philosophy

All kinds of development are happening throughout the entire body before it works. Your body remembers everything. You can't change unless you have your entire body working with you. It is so effective to practice silent yin, as well as special kinds of meditations that develop your senses and help you to get more grounded with your senses.

- It is important to have a grounded connection with the seasons, our natural cycle, diet and mindset.

- Your creativity is awakened and you're daring to believe what you feel. You start to find your own wisdom independent of other people.

- Instead of always taking care of everything, imagine your sensitivity as a strength.

- You can train your mindset, your habits, your body and senses with exercises designed to be sensitive.

- Find your way to live in freedom without reservations.

I have been training for many years and used my curiosity to develop tools that have helped me turn my sensitivity into my greatest strength.

People appreciate the tools they have been given, and these are all simple tools. They are deeply grateful when they find their own wisdom and figure out that highly sensitive is a strength.

It requires courage, but they feel happy when they are stepping up.

It is freedom.

If life is viewed as an adventure, you have the possibility of changing your habits to "a highly sensitive person with powerful senses."

My box is open now, and I am ready to share all my wisdom with you.

Now it is my time to rise, to share my passion and communicate my wisdom. I know that I am here to live an extraordinary life. I am sharing all my wisdom with you so you can discover how strong you are by using your sensitivity as a strength in your life.

Then you will find your inner peace and your inner beauty. You will find your own light.

Time to rise and shine.

My passion is to guide highly sensitive people to shine from their heart and let them find their inner power.

Let your life shine.

About the Author

Lene is a passionate transformational coach and teacher. She has developed a special kind of yoga called silent yin, silent relaxation and mindful living for highly sensitive people.

Lene's passion is to guide and help highly sensitive people to feel and find their inner power, and use their senses and nature as a strength to live a happy life.

Lene inspires sensitive people to train their mindset, habits, and their bodies to feel their inner power.

With all these tools, you have the opportunity to work with your consciousness in a deep way by listening to your heart and body.

Lene has a private practice with transforming communications for highly sensitive people, yoga and mindfulness training, combined with nature, courses, workshops and retreats.

Please contact:
www.mindmentor.dk
Email: info@mindmentor.dk
Lene Kirk – telephone +45 28812700
Denmark

Life is a Journey

Marijana Popovic

"What you think, you become. What you feel, you attract.
What you imagine, you create."

~ Buddha

I just finished working and decided to walk home through Battersea Park. London is completely different from Serbia, where I was born and raised. Here, people are always out and about, rushing around, but they rarely say hello, or nod, or smile to each other. What am I doing here? I wondered. I feel like I don't belong here. I decided then, to start smiling at everyone to see their reaction. To my surprise, some smiled back! Wow! But I'm getting ahead of myself. Let me go back few a year's...

I moved to London in July of 2008.

I grew up in a religious, traditional, patriarchal family in Tobolac, a small town in Serbia with my brother Marko, my mum Milanka, my dad Slavoljub and my cousin Tamara. In Tobolac, everybody knows each other, people are friendly and always ready to help; even strangers in the street. Everybody looks after each other and when you see stranger in the street you smile. Coming to London at the age of twenty-five was a massive shock to me. I had no friends or family. Why did I come to London? For love of course. I fell in love and followed my heart. Bojan was everything I was looking for: kind, funny, loved by friends and family. And he had impeccable manners, long hair and beautiful blue eyes. We dated from 2005 to 2008 when he finally convinced me to move to London.

I always compared my life in Serbia with my life in London.

In London, although I always tried to keep a smile on my face, deep down I wasn't happy. I missed my family and the friendly people of Serbia. In London, the only person, who knew the real me was, Bojan. He was very supportive during this period and he tried to be understanding but I was not the same person he'd met three years. I'd changed. I was angry, moody and depressed. But, I didn't tell this to anybody. I was stubborn and my ego wouldn't let me talk about my problems. I thought that I wasn't allowed to show my pain. When I was thirteen I told my mum: "I'm not feeling well. I think I'm getting my period." She replied, "Shut up! Are you going to complain every month for the rest of your life about this?" So, I learned to keep my pain inside me and to not talk about it. I know now this is wrong.

In June 2009 I discovered a book *The Secret* by Rhonda Byrnes. The premise was based on The Law of Attraction, about how we, by focusing on what we want in our life, can attract it and make it a reality. Rhonda outlined a three-step process to achieve it: ask, believe and receive. This is based on a Bible quote from Matthew 21:22: "And all things, whatsoever ye shall ask in prayer, believing, ye shall receive." Rhonda highlights the importance of gratitude and visualization in achieving our desires and how we can use it to have better relationships, health and to become prosperous. I was intrigued and decided to put the concepts into practice to attract positive energy into my life.

While I was focusing on this and trying to understand how to manifest it I learned a valuable lesson. I was finishing up at work, when my phone rang. When I answered I heard an old friend from Serbia say, "Don't worry, Marko is going to be fine. The best doctors in Belgrade are waiting to see him..." At that moment everything around me went black. Something had happened to my brother. With my heart racing I said, "What are you talking about?"

He responded, "Oh, you don't know... Marko had a car accident last night and... You'd better call your parents."

It was very hard time for me but I became very strong. I used the Law of Attraction to visualize my brother's recovery. I focused on him getting better. A few weeks after the accident Marko had a successful operation. My brother was safe! I realized how much better I'd felt after crying and letting all the pain out! The Law of Attraction had worked for me! Not for a second did I think Marko wouldn't make it. I focused all my energy on visualizing him getting better.

A year later I was still focusing on what I wanted in my life. My ego was still big but I was older and wiser. It was time to for me to get my permanent visa. After using the Law of Attraction and being successful with it, I became less religious and more spiritual. I realized that I was creating what was happening in my life and I started be more conscious about my thoughts. I believed I would get my visa and I did! I was over the moon! I'd been unhappy in my job for a while and decided that I would use the Law of Attraction to visualize a new one. I realized there were much more opportunities in London for me. I also wanted to have a baby. I told Bojan, and we went for our medical exams, and the results came back okay. We were very excited about having a baby.

In May 2011 I discovered a book *Rich Dad Poor Dad* by Robert Kiyosaki about all the possibilities open to us—that we only need to identify them and pursue them. Reading *Rich Dad Poor Dad* has changed my prospective about money. It advocates the importance of financial literacy, financial independence, and building wealth through investing in assets and real estate, starting and owning businesses, as well as increasing our financial intelligence to improve our business and financial aptitude. It inspired me to consider opening my own business and to also help people start their own business to pursue their passion. The only dark spot at this time was I was still not pregnant. Bojan arranged for us to see specialist.

I was told that I could not get pregnant because my AMH was low. AMH stands for Anti-Mullerian Hormone. It is also called MIS (Mullerian Inhibiting Substance). Since AMH is produced by the granulosa cells lining the ovarian follicles, AMH levels correlate with the number of antral follicles in the ovaries. The specialist suggested we try IVF. I was devastated and asked God why this was happening to me? I'm good person, I love kids and I wanted to have at least seven children! My passion was to be a teacher and work with students with special needs. Why is life treating me like this? Then I remembered the Law of Attraction and how it had helped me in the past and I decided to be positive and to visualize the outcome I wanted. I focused on the IVF working and on having a healthy baby. I also visualized a way to open my own business and what my business could be.

For the next two years I had two unsuccessful IVFs…

In the meantime, I decided to finish college in London and get a teaching degree. I was doing so much: working, studying, IVFs, and was starting to feel overwhelmed. During this time I discovered The Power Of Now By Eckhart Tolle, a self-help guide that stressed the importance of living in the present moment and avoiding thoughts of the past or future. This quote left an impact on me: "The most common ego identifications have to do with possessions, the work you do, social status and recognition, knowledge and education, physical appearance, special abilities, relationships, person and family history, belief systems, and often also political, nationalistic, racial, religious, and other collective identifications. None of these is you." The book taught me how to appreciate everyone and everything around me in the present moment and to also be conscious of my surroundings because it affects me more than I know. After reading it and after unsuccessful IVFs I decided to take a break to focus on teaching. I also joined a network of marketing companies to find out how to create a business of my own. I started learning about affiliate marketing; a marketing arrangement by which an online retailer pays commission to an external website for traffic or sales generated from its referrals which interested me because you can earn commission from $1 to $10000 depending on what product you are promoting. Also, you have a freedom to choose when you want to work and where you want to work. By the end of the year I had very nice passive income from it.

During this time I read another book, *The Monk Who Sold His Ferrari* by Robin Sharma. From it I learned that I have to receive, not only give. This was something I'd never thought about: the idea of getting and not just giving. This inspiring tale is based on the author's own search for life's true purpose, providing a step-by-step approach to living with greater courage, balance, abundance and joy. I started practicing being comfortable receiving from others. It was another life-changing moment. It was easier for me to learn new things because I was open to receiving knowledge and gifts, without feeling that I needed to give something in return.

In May 2016 I had learned all I could about affiliate marketing and I took an intensive course on Search Engine Optimization (SEO). I learned how to create websites and how to market them to "drive traffic" to the sites. It was given in a workshop with lodging at a bed and breakfast in the countryside. I found my peace and my knowledge in the one place. It was a wonderful community of professionals who knew the industry and had the skills I needed. They taught me that the best way to learn is from people who have done what they are teaching, can show the results of their experiences, and who are ready to share their knowledge.

After this course I started another round of IVF and I was now ready to "receive the gift" of a child.

July 2016

IFV is finished and on my birthday, July 27th, I received the greatest gift of all. I found out that I was pregnant! On 25th March 2017 I gave a birth to my beautiful, healthy, daughter Tara! When the doctor put her in my arms everything I'd gone through, all the pain of the IVFs and the worry, disappeared. The long journey to hold her, and every tear I'd shed became just a memory. During those painful years I had learned a lot and was able change myself and my life to be able to experience happiness.

In July 2017 we went to Serbia to see my family and to introduce them to Tara. We had a great time but something was bothering me. I faced one of the most painful decisions in my life: Should I throw away my dream to be an entrepreneur or should I be "practical" now that we had a baby to take care of? I was encouraged to "be responsible" and to "get a real job and forget about affiliate marketing." I know they meant well but they didn't understand that I was trying to make my dreams come true. I am the kind of person who likes to keep growing. I am uncomfortable when I feel limited. I wanted to make the best of myself so I could impact the world in a greater way. Deep down I didn't feel it was selfish to want this. I think it's our right to live our life in our own way. But that didn't stop friends and family from telling me I was wrong. Maybe they were projecting their fears onto me! I wondered if they were right. Maybe I should be "practical." But deep down in my heart I knew I deserved the life I wanted to live!

I also realized that I would not be able to leave my daughter in someone else's care to go back to work. I had fought for her for so long that I couldn't even comprehend being away from her all day. I want to be with her. I wanted to see all the changes she goes through as she grows and to be there for her.

I decided to open my own company, and to push forward against the odds. Instead of only teaching I decided to give lectures and workshops about affiliate marketing and share my knowledge. I felt 100 percent committed and I knew it was the right thing to do! That clarity led to incredible momentum in my business. In Aug 2017, I opened my own company as soon as we got back to London. This has also led to lots of speaking opportunities across the UK and internationally, about the world of Internet marketing. Having my own business gave me the flexibility and freedom to work at my passion and to raise my daughter. I had grown so much over the past 8 years and I now understand life better. I now know that why we must face hardships to learn the lessons we need to grow. I had to wait to have a perfect, healthy, smart, beautiful baby because I was not ready to be a mum. I first had to find myself and my purpose before I could have Tara, and also to be strong enough to start my own business.

Life is a journey. It's not a straight line. There are twists and turns and we must be able to take the ups and downs and learn from them. I know that I am so blessed now, because of the hardships I faced. They allowed me to become the person I needed to be to receive my blessings.

Today, I am fortunate to have taught many clients and the strategies I teach are vetted and proven. I now talk about the events that got me where I am now and my experiences have helped a number of my clients who were ready to make changes in their personal, and business, life. Tara is my inspiration! She always gets her moment on the stage. She is my WHY and also my HOW. What I do is for her, but I am able to do it, because of her.

It's not easy to be a full-time mum and entrepreneur, to work with clients, and also have a family life. But I did it. If your heart beats for something you'll find a way to live your passion. My heart was beating for the life I wanted so I created it. I merged my passion with my personal and work life. I now decide when I want to work, when I want to go on holiday, and when I want to go for a walk with my family. I have the freedom to choose. You can too! If somebody tells you "you can't do it" just smile, walk away, and then prove them wrong…because you can!

About the Author

My name is Marijana Popovic, I was born in Serbia July 27th, 1983. I lived in Tobolac until 2008 when I moved to London. Now, I am a full time mum to Tara, and also an entrepreneur. I have a passion for helping people change direction and live the life they deserve (just like I did), I provide coaching, workshops, and training to help you achieve your financial goals.

Please visit my website and feel free to contact me if you think there is anything I can help you with.
http://mumentrepreneur.company

Free From Labels

Elaine Mendoza

I was done. Life, as I knew it, was over. I had this realization as I sat in my apartment, exhausted from another twelve-hour workday. I was living in a lavish apartment that I did not have time to enjoy. I was trading my life for money and that is the poorest return on our most valuable investment: our time. I was waking up with night sweats and a draining anxiety. As I sat up in bed, an inner voice would whisper, "This is not the life you are supposed to be living." I quieted the voice by becoming a workaholic and overeating.

I can almost sense my spirit pre-birth, gambling with my life and placing a bet as to how destiny would turn out for me. The term "Shakespearean tragicomedy" stuck with me as an appropriate label for my life. First of all, I was born into a Catholic family with the equivalent of Mother Teresa as a mother. My father? A Venezuelan version of Dr. Sigmund Freud. I recall stories of him making my older siblings—three of them also gay—write in a notebook "I am not gay," over and over, until they were "healed" of their "homosexuality." You can imagine my surprise when my crushes on boys in the sixth grade changed in the seventh grade to the girls in my class. Like Cinderella, I wanted a better life for myself, but I was completely disinterested in going to the ball. I had to create a new story because there were no role models for kids like me. I was not going to be saved by a handsome prince. I had to take responsibility for my own fate.

From the moment we are born, there are labels that people use to describe us. Whether we are black, white, Latino, Asian, and so on, these labels now cause friction and sometimes hatred between human beings. Something that describes us is now keeping us separated from each other. I realized that being who I was, from my Nationality to my Sexuality, was dangerous, shameful, and not something to be shared. The labels were also fighting each other within *me*. For example, could I still believe in Christ *and* be attracted to women? Catholicism was teaching me that I was not welcome, unless I healed my sexual tendencies. The desire was okay, but I could not act on it. And if I was attracted to women could I also date men, or should I label myself into another box? Even the gay and lesbian community judged those that did not identify as strictly one or another. Anything that would vary from the "norm" would be dismissed as confusion or living in denial.

My survival instincts were on overdrive and it was too much for my psyche and spirit. I decided to become many other people through the performing arts. After all, everyone loves a performer. It was safe for me to express my very complex emotions through theater classes, singing lessons, and on the stage with my classmates. The emotions were real, but they were carefully expressed through the mask that were characters, and fantasies, on the stage.

My self-deprecating and dismissive sense of humor helped me get through my obstacles like a quiet observer of the events in my life. Somehow, it minimized the severity of the issues that I had to face. I was not even aware of how depressed I was as a teen and young adult. No one would have suspected that jumping off a cliff was one of my many fantasies until I realized that there was humor in the word cliff. I was a QLIF (queer, Latina, immigrant, and female). However, I did not yet live in a world where it was safe to be me, and the hardest obstacles I would face was to be everything that I already was.

I am the summation of four minorities embodied in one person and no matter where I searched for love and approval, there was someone rejecting me. I would turn on the television only to hear how immigrants were taking all the jobs. I wondered how everyone was taking jobs without work permits. I listened to the radio and heard how gay marriage was an abomination while having a partner in the hospital that I could not add to my health insurance like my heterosexual coworkers. I heard that women were making less than men for the same job, while listening to, racist and stereotypical comments about my ethnicity. Even turning to my family wasn't an option because I already knew what my parents would put me through. My older siblings had already lived it. What happens when it feels like all the hate and rejection of the world feels like it is directed at YOU?

Who decided that some human beings were more worthy of love, respect, equal rights, and a sense of humanity than others? Why are some people treated differently depending on their race, nationality, religion, sexuality, and so on? Simply being who I was put me at risk for neglect, discrimination, hatred, and constant rejection, not just from my parents and family, but society in general. It's no wonder that I had ulcers by the time I was twenty-one. Later on, I developed severe endometriosis. Everything I was hiding was literally eating my insides. What we do not express, we literally depress until it becomes noticeable through full blown depression and physical illness. The mind/body connection was evident. My body was already aware of my hidden fears and feelings until it forced me to pay attention to myself. I'm not saying that every illness is something that we intentionally manifest. I'm acknowledging that repressing whom we are reveals itself as anxiety, sadness, and depression. We can only hide for so long and after a prolonged matter of time it takes a toll on our mental and physical health.

Depression and sadness were so normal to me in my young adult life that I didn't really know what "feeling good" meant. I found escape through unhealthy lovers, obsessed with my weight, and anything that I felt I could control. But deep down, I knew that metaphorically, I was in a car going 100 mph and some day I would crash. And crash I did. The crash was not what you would think. It was only an illusion created by the labels we give ourselves and the power of fear over our existence.

Eventually, I did become a U.S. citizen and achieved The American Dream that I had been desperately chasing most of my life. I had the security of a stable job as a train conductor that allowed me to travel, but not to the extent that I wanted to. I had an apartment by the water, and a career that could easily make me a six-figure income if I put in enough overtime. I no longer had the immigration or personal obstacles of the past. I was out to family and friends without their need for approval or affirmation. On the surface everything looked fine, but I still felt like something wasn't right. I felt I had replaced one prison with another. The first prison I inherited, but the second one I created. The choice was ultimately mine.

We all have labels that imprison us, yet we are the only ones that can find our true path. Like most people, I had fallen into fulfilling society's expectations. I told myself that if I only worked harder I would make the money I needed to do what I really wanted to do. I started talking to coworkers on the verge of retirement only to realize that I didn't want to give my life away for one I would regret. I did not have any coworkers who felt their lives were fully lived. On the contrary, they had sacrificed all those years on the railroad to collect a pension plan in their golden years. Several of them would not even live long enough to enjoy the pension they had sacrificed their lives for.

My work days were long and I only had one day off a week. Eventually, this inner voice became louder. Change isn't easy. It is actually quite painful. I now realized that I had to give up my stable job for the unknown. I could not ignore the health issues that I would have because of that job. It would have been a matter of time before I needed my knees replaced or my shoulder readjusted. I had to give up a routine, that no matter how much I disliked it, it was safe. Emotionally, long days at work while sacrificing time with loved ones would also catch up with me. I had to trust that the same forces that were pushing me out into the unknown would be the same forces that would help me transition into a new life. I decided to take that leap of faith.

I resigned on Valentine's Day 2015 as a metaphor to my self-love. I quit the job that provided the apartment, the car, and the steady paycheck, to embrace the unknown. However, I also quit the job that was taking my life away in exchange for a paycheck. Now, I had all the time in the world to simply be. I had built a life based on fear. Imagine the life that I could create out of inspiration, love, and joy! After living in immigration hell for so long, which kept me trapped in The United States, I decided that I wanted to experience as many faraway lands as possible. And I did just that. I yelled PROUST while drinking with strangers at Oktoberfest in Germany. I walked the romantic streets of Venice while eating the best gelato in town.

I sang tunes from *The Sound of Music* while I visited Salzburg. The gorgeous beaches of Thailand nourished my soul, and the inspiring music in Prague reignited my urge to sing. I did not just feel my essence, I WAS this energy, and it was pure happiness. It is easy to get into contact with your true self when you are no longer a Nationality, a Sexuality, an employee, a sister, a daughter, a lover, a woman over thirty with a single status, and so on. One by one I noticed all the labels peel off into nothingness, but I also found myself there. I started having extraordinary realizations that I was writing in a journal which later turned into a book.

I was free to start rebuilding from a place that supported what made me happy while tossing out what did not support my peace of mind or my joy. I did not know what was in store for me or what would come of all of this. I just knew that I could no longer live my life in shame or fear. I could no longer relate to old ways of thinking, living, and a complete lack of just *being*. I was still an immigrant, Latina, female, and queer so what had changed? *I had changed*. I had internalized this message that I was not worthy of more because I was all of these "labels." You may not be an immigrant, queer, female or a person of color. However, I bet there are labels that YOU are holding on to that are making you a prisoner of your own life. Perhaps you are a prisoner of your beliefs. Maybe you don't feel worthy of a better life, job, or marriage. Now when I look at my life, I simply can't believe that in three years I went from being "on call" 24/7, to working in my pajamas in front of my computer. See, it was never about the money, prestige, relationships, or even my immigration status. Once I became free of living inside a box, which is true for most of us—I was able to create a life full of freedom, joy, and endless possibilities. As a traveler, I believe that the more we engage with people who are different from us, and share who we intrinsically are with them, the more we will start to see our differences as gifts to the world. The labels that we use to keep each other separated no longer ring true. It *is* possible to live in a world without labels, but first we must remove the ones that are currently taking control of our lives.

Nowadays, I rotate my life between the U.S., Playa del Carmen, Mexico, and Europe. I create retreats for people to be able to experience for themselves the places, adventures, and meals that have enriched my life. I teach languages online, and I write travel articles and blogs. I have been published in a travel magazine, and corporations hire me to write blog posts for them. I have been invited to speak about my experiences. Finally, I am performing again for Playa Pride—the pride events of Playa del Carmen and for the Prague Multicultural Music Project. I am also a supporter of ZamDance---A non-profit dance program for kids with disabilities. Imagine, all the talents that were already within me are now out in the open. My degree in Musical Theater is finally being put to use.

How poetic to define this chapter of my life by drinking amazing Mexican coffee at The Choux Choux Cafe in Playa del Carmen, while drafting my first book. Five years ago, no one could have predicted this. Not even me. The Mayan energy and the magical atmosphere of this side of the world welcomes me and accompanies me on this journey. My website, FinallyElaine.com, documents everything. It is my personal space that I share with everyone.

Three years ago, "they" said I should not, but I *have*. "They" said I cannot, but I *will*. They said I will not, but I *did*. Never let others tell you what you can or cannot do. *You*, define, *you*.

About the Author

Elaine Mercedes Mendoza's family moved from Venezuela to The United States in 1980. She studied Visual Media and Literature at American University in Washington D.C. and Musical Theater at A.M.D.A. NY. However, not being born in The United States kept her life in limbo until 2007 when she was finally able to pursue a life like every other native born citizen. The challenges of the past encouraged her to create a life full of travels and freedom.

Passionate about the planet we are creating, a location independent lifestyle was a natural fit. In her spare time, Elaine loves to sing for a cause, speak to others about her previous obstacles and overcoming them, and is a social activist for immigrants, Latin-Americans, women, and the LGBTQ community. She runs FinallyElaine.com and loves promoting an inclusive world without labels. She is grateful for her amazing friends all over the world.

Connect with Elaine Online:
www.FinallyElaine.com
www.facebook.com/finallyelaine/

Finding My 'Why'

Sarah K Brandis

Twenty-eight might sound like a strange age to have an existential crisis, but I didn't really 'do life' in the traditional order anyway! Here's a little story about accidentally finding my purpose while pursuing a different path entirely…

When I was growing up, I never really knew what I wanted to be. Sure, I had lots of interests; animals, space, travel, science, and more animals. But I didn't have a vision for the sort of work I would do, and I don't think I really believed that I was capable of much.

When I first left home at sixteen years old, the struggle of surviving in the real world of adult responsibilities hit me like a tidal wave. I was so overwhelmed with just taking care of myself, finding a place to live and paying for it, that I didn't think too much about the type of work I took on.

Without a role model, or a guiding hand (that didn't have its own agenda), my early twenties were a blur of bad decisions.

At twenty-six I made the 'bold decision' to marry the guy I'd been dating for only six months before he asked me. Looking back, this decision was beyond reckless. Neither of us were in a good place mentally, nor were we prepared to really be adults.

But you know, I think a lot of people have fallen into that particular trap. When you are a bit lost in this world, it's natural to cling to the first person who shows you some love. Whether they are good for you, or not. He needed someone to look after him, calm his drink-induced tantrums and help pay the bills. I needed to be needed, and I wanted to belong somewhere more than anything at that time.

So, we did the deed, and we lasted through 18 months of emotional tugs of war, before the explosive finale. I was the one to pull the plug. It came after I broke down at work, in a job where I was bullied by my angry, cocaine-fueled manager.

My husband reacted to my breakdown with anger, making it all about him. In short, the response was 'how dare I have problems.' He was the one who needed to be looked after. It couldn't work both ways.

That complete lack of support was the deal-breaker for me. I realized then that he didn't love *me*, he loved what I could do for him. If I wasn't being his caretaker, I was somehow in the wrong.

Although getting married to him was a terrible idea, there was something both cathartic and important for me about getting divorced. It was rather symbolic for me; symbolic of claiming my life back, and of putting myself first, and maybe for the first time, too.

Looking back, I know that this experience, like all my others, was a part of what led me to my breaking point. If I hadn't had wasted so much time being looking after him, I might not have become frustrated enough to change the direction of my life.

The truth is, if I hadn't been in that marriage and learned that lesson about putting myself first, then I probably wouldn't have even dreamed that I could do something just for myself. I used to do the 'right thing' by everyone else, and that had included paying the bills. This was going to be the first time I'd given myself the green light to be 'selfish.'

I still didn't have any good role models in my life at the time. And now I really understand how crucial this is for living your best life. The absence of a good example, plus a lack of belief in myself, really slowed down my decision to change things. I don't know if it's exactly true that we are the sum of the five people we spend the most time with. But I get where that belief comes from, and it makes a lot of sense.

Certainly, if we surround ourselves with negativity then it rubs off on us. And conversely, when we spend time with people who lift us up, we become more like them, and we see more opportunity for ourselves. Not only that—when you ask a positive person for support, you get it in spades. Quite a difference!

Back at the time of my existential crisis, I think the person I looked up to the most was my manager at work. He'd been kind to me. In fact, he's been my manager before in two other companies. When he got his new job there, he invited me along and gave me a job there too, which got me away from my cocaine-fueled bully of a manager. And I was so grateful.

I think the struggle here came for me when I saw that he wasn't happy in his new role. He was fairly despondent, truth be told, and didn't do anything about it. That really confused me, and to be honest, it kind of made me angry. I hated seeing somebody that I looked up to being, well, kind of helpless. I know this sounds selfish, but I wanted him to give me hope, not show me what it looked like to be miserable.

So we started to clash, big time. Every time he would overlook something that could make our department run better, I got mad at him. The growing gap between us was one of the reasons I used to cry at work every day. This was so uncomfortable, and it couldn't be all there was to life, surely? Was I really to understand that the most I could hope for was to dread work before it started, hate it while I was there, and be tired and sad when I got home?

The rage was growing in me like a tumor; it got a little bit denser every day, and it was making me sick. If it didn't come out soon, it would take me down with it.

The peak of my existential crisis came on an ordinary workday. I was sitting at my desk—the one I was supposed to be working at! But I didn't care about my work anymore. And to be fair, my manager didn't care if I was working either. Sure, my job paid the bills, but it also made me cry nearly every day. I was flat, deflated, like somebody had pulled my stopper out, and my 'air' was escaping.

The strongest feeling was resentment. I hated that my full-time working hours, such a big chunk of my waking time on earth, was spent grinding for somebody else's purpose, not my own. But honestly, I didn't know what mine was.

So rather than being compelled to change by a glittery, shiny dream, I was pushed to change by my personal pain. Les Brown says that's what happens for most people. They don't get out of their rut until there is enough pain to push them out.

To be honest, this was a pattern I was repeating. This is just the same as what I had let happen with my husband. I waited until things were unbearable before I made a change.

The essence of an existential crisis is the big question, "why am I here." And I don't just mean, why I was there at my desk on that day. I mean, why was I on earth? What did my existence mean? I didn't have a 'why,' a purpose, or a reason.

When daily survival takes over, the 'big questions' fly out of view. You live from week to week, paycheck to paycheck. Dreams seem so far out of reach. Living is for 'one day.' I seemed to exist only to pay my bills.

I'd snapped, but in a really good way! My focus had shifted from one day to TODAY, and I was ready to make a big change. So the question now was, *where was I going to go with this?* I needed some inspiration.

At the time, I was sharing a flat with my friend Karin. Although I loved her dearly, I have to admit that I was a bit envious of her life. She had a great family, financial and emotional support, and although she was studying at university, she'd already pinned down an awesome job before graduating.

I had always felt like I'd 'missed out' on university, as it's something that most people do with the support of their parents. And I loved learning. I'd actually taken an Open University correspondence course in the past (while working full-time) and I'd really enjoyed it. So why not treat myself to something the 'lucky' kids take for granted? I could manage without support; I just needed a student loan and a part-time job.

At the Open University, I had taken a certificate in basic psychology. The human mind had always been one of my fascinations, and I loved the idea of working in a helping profession. So when I found a university near me in London that offered a degree in Cognitive Neuroscience, it was a no-brainer, and also the worst pun ever.

Fortunately for me, my existential crisis came at the ideal time of year to apply for a university place. My interview came around quite quickly, and I was so excited in the meeting room that I don't think the interviewer dared to turn me down. This was happening. Yet waiting for term to start, and my full-time job to end, was so slow. I crossed the days off my calendar like a prisoner marking her days off on the cell wall.

The four years I spent at university were amazing. I'd never before experienced the feeling of doing something so big that was just for me. I loved almost every minute, barring a few exam-related freak-outs and the countdown to handing in my dissertation.

And then I graduated. It was a triumph and a comedown all at the same time. On the one hand, I was so proud of myself and happy that I'd made it. On the other hand, I was being ejected back into the land of full-time work and adult responsibilities. *Hadn't I already done that? Hadn't I escaped once before?* Damn, here I went again!

The toughest part was deciding what to do. Sure, I could work in almost any low-paid, unskilled job like I had before. I wouldn't starve. But I didn't want to slide backward. I'd just spent four years and an exorbitant amount of student finance on leveling up. So I had to figure out how to make that count in the real world.

I had this vague idea about helping people in a psychological capacity. I had counseling when I was in my early twenties, and it had not only helped me, but inspired me too. So I was thinking about this sort of work for myself.

I started a life coaching course with a company that I found online. It was interesting, but not quite what I had expected. I wasn't sure that coaching was really for me, although I loved to be coached by the other students and enjoyed the general vibe of being around other people who also wanted to help in this world.

Several months into my training, the founder of the school put out a post on Facebook that they were looking for someone to help with marketing. Now, this wasn't a career that I had considered before, but I did have some relevant experience—plus, I was really curious if this might be something I'd enjoy.

Back at university, I'd decided to tick something off of my bucket list. You might recall me saying that I'd left home at sixteen with no support. Well, no surprise, there is a story there. I had toyed with the idea of writing a book about my experiences for many years. Up until my student days, this was nothing more than a bunch of scrappy notes tucked into a blue folder that I took with me each time I moved houses. But it was going to be something someday.

So, while I was studying, I made use of the big, end-of-term holidays to knuckle down and write my book.

It was only once I self-published my work that I realized the importance of marketing. A few shares from my social media profiles weren't going to get my book into the charts. To make a long story short, I took a few online marketing courses in my spare time and learned how to make my book visible. At one point during a free promo period, I got to number one in the mental health charts. This was when I felt the immense pride of a job well done, and I also felt the awesome power of a marketing campaign done right. It was love! Sarah the marketer was born.

Accidental discoveries might just be the best ones! Sometimes the best-laid plans are born of our 'shoulds,' or driven by our brain rather than our hearts. So, I'm really glad that I accidentally stumbled into my purpose, as I know my brain didn't get a chance to interrupt my heart. It all just happened, and it always felt right.

Although I always had a sense that I would be helping people, I had thought that it would be more about helping in a 'healthcare' way, not with marketing their small businesses.

I have my 'why' now, and it's helping small business owners to get their dreams off the ground. I love empowering people, and I think the value of what I do is less about the practical skills I teach (although those certainly help) and more about giving clients the confidence to say, "Hey, it's doable!" So, I guess I'm still helping from a psychological angle too!

And now that I have a small business myself, and I've taken that scary leap of building something new from scratch, I can say the following with some authority.

Screw following the 'traditional order' of life. You get this lifetime once and it's happening now. Right now. If you're ready to rise, then please, start rising as soon as you can. You don't have to wait for the pain to push you. It's your time to rise whenever you decide it is. And you certainly don't have to follow the crowd. Make yourself happy!

A bit of parting advice...

If you're stuck, get a role model or a mentor. I have four right now, and you know, three of them probably don't even know they are my role models. That's the thing; you don't have to hire an expert for guidance. Awesome people are all around us, if we look.

Choose someone who inspires you to live your best life. Someone who lifts you up and encourages you to reach a little further, to be brave, and above all, to be happy. We all need a little guidance sometimes.

About the Author

Sarah K. Brandis is a writer and social media trainer based in London, UK.

Her mission is to empower other solopreneurs to follow their dreams by teaching them copy writing, content and social media made as simple as possible.

In her free time, she enjoys running, nature, and is mildly obsessed with her three cats.

Say hello here: <u>sarahkbrandis.com</u>

Find me at: <u>sarahkbrandis.com</u>

About the Book's Creator

<u>Dr. Andrea Pennington</u> is an integrative physician, acupuncturist, meditation teacher, and sex educator who is on a mission to raise the level of consciousness and love on our planet. She has provided holistic healthcare to men and women for over seventeen years and now provides personal and professional development programs for healers, coaches, Light workers and change makers. As a renowned personal brand architect, media producer, and communications specialist, she leverages her 20 + years of experience in broadcast and digital media to proudly help people bring their brilliance to the world through publishing and media production with <u>Make Your Mark Global Media</u>.

Dr. Andrea is also a bestselling author, international TEDx speaker, documentary filmmaker, and sought-after media personality. For nearly two decades, Dr. Andrea has shared her candid, empowering insights on vitality and resilience on the *Oprah Winfrey Show*, the *Dr. Oz Show*, iTV *This Morning*, CNN, the *Today Show*, LUXE-TV, Thrive Global and HuffingtonPost and as a news anchor for Discovery Health Channel. She also produced a four-part documentary series and DVD for Gaia entitled *Simple Steps to a Balanced Natural Pregnancy*.

Dr. Andrea has appeared in several newspapers, magazines including *Essence, Ebony, Newsweek, The Sun, Red*, and *Stylist*. She has also written or contributed to 10 books. Now as host of the daily talk show, *Liberate Your Authentic Self* on the America Out Loud talk radio platform, she brings her insight and inspiration for purposeful living, conscious relationships and soulful success. And as host of Sensual Vitality-TV she brings her unique "nerdy" blend of medical science, positive psychology, and mindfulness meditation, to empower women to show up authentically, love passionately, and live orgasmically.

261

Visit Dr. Andrea online at:

AndreaPennington.com, www.RealSelf.Love and MakeYourMarkGlobal.com

Get Social!

https://www.facebook.com/DrAndreaPennington
https://twitter.com/drandrea
https://www.linkedin.com/in/andreapennington
https://www.instagram.com/drandreapennington/

Other Books Published by Make Your Mark Global

I Love You, Me! My Journey to Overcoming Depression and Finding Real Self-Love Within by Andrea Pennington

The Orgasm Prescription for Women: 21 Days to Heightened Pleasure, Deeper Intimacy and Orgasmic Bliss by Andrea Pennington

The Book on Quantum Leaps for Leaders: The Practical Guide to Becoming a More Efficient and Effective Leader from the Inside Out by Bitta. R. Wiese

Turning Points: 11 Inspiring True Stories of Turning Life's Challenges into a Driving Force for Personal Transformation by A Collection of Coaches & Mentors, Compiled by Andrea Pennington

How to Liberate and Love Your Authentic Self by Andrea Pennington

The Top 10 Traits of Highly Resilient People by Andrea Pennington

Daily Compassion Meditation: 21 Guided Meditations,

Quotes and Images to Inspire Love, Joy and Peace by Andrea Pennington

Eat to Live: Protect Your Body + Brain + Beauty with Food by Andrea Pennington

MAKE YOUR MARK GLOBAL

Get Published Share Your Message with the World

Make Your Mark Global is a branding, marketing and communications agency based in the USA and French Riviera/Monaco. We offer publishing, content development, and promotional services to heart-based, conscious authors who wish to have a lasting impact through the sharing and distribution of their transformative message. We can also help authors build a strong online media presence and platform for greater visibility.

If you'd like help writing, publishing, or promoting your book, or if you'd like to co-author a collaborative book, visit us online or call for a free consultation. Call +1 (707) 776-6310 or send an email to andrea@MakeYourMarkGlobal.com
www.MakeYourMarkGlobal.com